IN *Life* AND IN *Death*

A Pastoral Guide for Funerals

Written and compiled by
Leonard J. Vander Zee

Grand Rapids, Michigan

10 9 8 7 6 5 4

Library of Congress-in-Publications Data

Vander Zee, Leonard J., 1945—
In life and in death : a pastoral guide for funerals / written and compiled by Leonard J. Vander Zee.
p. cm.
ISBN 978-1-56212-022-1
1. Funeral service—Texts. 2. Christian Reformed Church—Liturgy—Texts. 3. Reformed Church—Liturgy—Texts. 4. Church work with the bereaved.
I. Title
BX9575.F8V35 1992 92-17841
264".057310985—dc20 CIP

What is your only comfort
in life and in death?

That I am not my own,
but belong—
    body and soul,
    in life and in death—
to my faithful Savior Jesus Christ.

—Heidelberg Catechism Q & A 1

Key to Sources of Prayers and Readings

ASB: *The Alternative Service Book* 1980
BCP: *The Book of Common Prayer*
BS: *The Book of Services*
CGP: *Canticles and Gathering Prayers*
KJV: *Holy Bible: King James Version*
LBW: *Lutheran Book of Worship*
NIV: *Holy Bible: New International Version*
OCF: *Order of Christian Funerals*
OS: *Occasional Services*
PDC: *Prayers for the Domestic Church*
PsH: *Psalter Hymnal*
SMT: *Proposed Services of Memorial and Thanksgiving*
TF: *The Funeral: A Service of Witness to the Resurrection*
UCA: *Uniting Church Worship Services: Funeral*

Further information on these sources is available in the Acknowledgments section on page 219. All prayers not credited were written by Leonard J. Vander Zee.

Contents

Foreword

In the Christian Reformed Church (CRC), funeral services have been "uncharted territory" until now. Never before has the denomination developed any resources for use by those who are called to plan and conduct funerals. *In Life and in Death* began with a 1986 mandate from the CRC Publications Board to the denominational Liturgical Committee (now, CRC Worship Committee) to "develop a model (or models) for funeral services."

As committee members began their study, they became convinced that the churches needed more than service models. A whole complex of pastoring needs surround a funeral, such as praying with one who is near death or comforting the family of one who has just died. So in 1988 the CRC Publications Board approved an expanded proposal—the seed from which this manual grew. In addition to the services, pastoral advice and many prayers and readings are offered here for those who seek to minister to persons who are near death as well as to families and friends who gather together at the time of a funeral.

Leonard J. Vander Zee, member of the CRC Worship Committee and pastor of the South Bend (Indiana) Christian Reformed Church, is the primary author and compiler of these resources. The historical introduction was written by Melvin D. Hugen, professor of pastoral care at Calvin Theological Seminary, Grand Rapids, Michigan. The chapter on pastoral care includes guidelines which were first developed by James R. Kok, Director of Pastoral Care at the Crystal Cathedral, Garden Grove, California. The chapter on music was written by LeRoy G. Christoffels, pastor of the Preakness Christian Reformed

Church, Wayne, New Jersey, and also a member of the Worship Committee.

We hope that these resources will be helpful to pastors and others who are called upon to comfort the mourning and to conduct the kinds of services that give testimony to the hope of the resurrection and the love of the Christian community.

The CRC Worship Committee (1991)

Jo Alberda	David Diephouse	Leonard Vander Zee
Wayne Brouwer	Linda Male	Emily Brink, *Editor*
LeRoy Christoffels	Bert Polman	
Dale Cooper	Tony Van Zanten	

Preface

A few years ago I stood with my wife and her family at the bedside of her dying father in a nursing home. He had suffered a massive stroke and was now slowly sinking toward death. While his labored breathing grew shallower and more infrequent, we waited, mostly silent, for death to come. As is usually the case in such situations, death arrived on silent feet, with no fanfare. One moment there was a barely alive person, the next, a lifeless body. The moment was no less awesome for its near imperceptibility.

After a few moments of silence, tears and hugs, and a prayer, we notified the nurse and began to make some preliminary preparations. We were informed that the funeral director would not arrive for an hour or two. As we waited, my brother-in-law, who is Russian Orthodox, suggested that we follow his tradition, which prescribes that at the moment of death a continuous reading of the Psalms commence. So someone picked up Dad's tattered old Bible and began to read Psalm 1. And we continued to read one psalm after another, passing the Bible around the group.

At first I assumed that this was merely a pious way of passing time. But very soon we were all powerfully drawn into the words of the psalms as they began to reflect Dad's life, his faith, his struggles, his destiny. It was almost uncanny how each new psalm led us through the memories and emotions that we needed to explore as we began that long process of grieving. I think we made it to Psalm 40 or so by the time the funeral director finally arrived, and we left off the reading with some reluctance.

It was that experience that led me to begin reflecting on and evaluating our practices surrounding death within the Christian Reformed community. The truth is that we offer little in the way of guidance for ministering to dying people or to the bereaved. Because our Church Order specifically excludes death and funerals from ecclesiastical concern, we have walled off dying and death from the rest of church life. We have labeled funerals as family matters—which indeed they are. But without some guidance, families and church communities may flounder at these important moments and may miss profound experiences of comfort and grace.

When someone close to us dies, we tend to fall into habitual actions and patterns that may or may not fit our needs. We look for words and gestures that will express the tangled feelings that fill our minds and hearts. Unfortunately, these practices may more often be dictated by expedience and local funeral customs than by the thoughtful guidance of the Christian community.

The more I struggled with these thoughts and experiences, the more convinced I became of the need for our own community of faith to fill this void. So when the CRC Worship Committee, of which I am a member, began to plan for a funeral manual, I expressed an interest in writing and compiling material for it.

This manual is written with the hope that pastors, elders, church musicians, and all the people of our communities of faith may learn to minister to dying and grieving people more effectively. I am grateful to Melvin Hugen and LeRoy Christoffels for the sections they wrote; to the CRC Worship Committee and Emily Brink for giving me this opportunity and for their patience, encouragement, and thoughtful suggestions. I also thank my wife, Judith, our children, Renee, Marie, Lenore, and Anton, and Judith's mother, Thressa Vroon, for their patience and encouragement, and especially for the opportunity to spend a month at Desert House of Prayer in Tucson, Arizona, working on this project.

And to all of you—when that inevitable moment arrives, may you sense with Dietrich Bonhoeffer that this is "not the end, but the beginning of life."

Leonard J. Vander Zee
Epiphany, 1991

INTRODUCTION

Funerals in the Christian and Reformed Tradition

Melvin D. Hugen

We all have pictures in our minds of what should and should not occur at a funeral. We acknowledge that most of our practices have been shaped by tradition or experience (we were comforted by one type of ceremony and found another jarring or unsettling). Some of our customs have been shaped by the world around us; others have deep roots in the history of Christ's church.

Early Church

Unlike many of their pagan contemporaries, the early Christians did not regard a funeral as simply, or even primarily, an occasion of mourning. They saw it rather as an opportunity to bear witness to the hope of the resurrection—to celebrate the fact that "Christ has indeed been raised from the dead, the firstfruits of those who have fallen asleep" (1 Cor. 15:20). For the believer in Christ, "death has been swallowed up in victory" (1 Cor. 15:54). The prevailing tone of these early funerals, therefore, was one of joyful thanksgiving. White was the dominant color, symbolizing the robes of purity worn by the multitude of the redeemed in heaven (Rev. 7:9-17).

These first Christian funerals were probably very simple affairs. Over time, however, a common structure emerged, consisting of three basic elements. First came prayers at the home of the deceased as the body was being prepared for burial. Next, the body was carried in procession to the place of worship for a service of praise, prayer, and Scripture, culminating in the celebration of the Lord's Supper, which signified the communion of the saints "at all times and in all places." The event was concluded with the interment, often followed by a fellowship meal.

Though these three elements were altered and elaborated on during the Middle Ages, largely due to monastic influences, this basic structure survived into the Reformation era. However, the *tone* of the services changed dramatically. The original sense of celebration, the joy of triumph over death, was replaced by a new emphasis on human mortality, the terrors of divine judgment, and the sinner's need for priestly absolution. Songs of praise and thanksgiving gave way to the *Dies Irae* ("Day of Wrath"); burial rites became the capstone of a vast penitential edifice, associated with extreme unction, purgatory, and propitiatory masses for the dead.

The Reformed Tradition

To the Protestant reformers these funeral practices seemed to typify the worst of the Roman church's theological abuses. And their antipathy to such "superstition" helps explain much of the subsequent history of funerals in the Reformed tradition. Rather than attempting to reform the existing ceremonies and practices—as Luther did, for example—John Calvin and his followers made no provision for funeral services of any kind. The rule of the churches of Geneva (1541) stated simply:

> The dead are to be buried decently in the place appointed. The attendance and company are left to each man's discretion. It will be good that the carriers be warned by us to discourage all superstitions contrary to the Word of God . . . .

Variations of this rule were adopted by Calvinists in England (Puritans), Scotland (Presbyterians), Ireland, France, Germany, and the Netherlands.

These provisions, however, were not rigidly followed, even by the reformers themselves. In a letter to Farel, Calvin approved giving an appropriate sermon in the churchyard after the burial. And as early as 1533, the first synod of Strassburg protested the custom of no services at the grave and asked that at least a pastor be present for the burial. Later synods, recognizing the practices of the patriarchs of the Old Testament and of the New Testament churches, adopted orders of service appropriate for burial. These simple orders recommended the use of Scripture readings, an exhortation, silent or free prayer, and the giving of alms.

But such concessions were not universally accepted. The Church Order of Dort (1618-1619), adopted for the Reformed churches of Scotland and the continent, stated:

> Funeral sermons (or services) shall not be introduced. In those places where they have already been introduced, diligent efforts must be made to abolish them in the most appropriate manner.

The Westminster Directory of the Church of Scotland (1644) was even more explicit:

> When any person departeth this life, let the dead body, upon the day of burial, be decently attended from the house to the place appointed for public burial, and there immediately interred, without any ceremony. And because the customs of kneeling down, and praying by, or towards the dead corpse, and other such usages, in the place where it lies, before it be carried to burial are superstitious; and for that, praying, reading, both going to and at the grave, have been grossly abused, are in no way beneficial to the dead, and have proved many ways hurtful to the living, therefore let all such things be laid aside.

Such rulings didn't succeed in eliminating funerals. Rather, they ensured that the practices or ceremonies used at the burial of Reformed Christians were shaped not by the church but by local custom and family tradition. Services, particularly in France and the Netherlands, were held at the grave and sometimes also in the church. But they were viewed as family ceremonies, similar to weddings, rather than as ecclesiastical services.

Interestingly, although the Reformed churches did little or nothing with the development of funeral rites and services, in some areas they had a strong tradition of preparation for and contemplation of death. For example, in many of their books on piety, the English Puritans included meditations on "holy dying": "When thou seest the bed, let it put thee in mind of the grave which is now the bed of Christ" (Lewis Bayly, *The Practice of Piety*, 1632). Perhaps this sort of meditation is the source of "If I should die before I wake," a phrase from a familiar child's prayer. The Reformed churches of the Netherlands (Hervormed) also provided a listing of readings and prayers entitled *Die Ziekentroost* (for the comfort of the sick), which included Scripture passages linked by comments intended to be read by or to the mortally ill and Scriptures to be read as prayers at the hour of death, the final one being, "Lord, into your hands I commit my spirit."

Since funerals, unlike the sacraments, are not commanded by the Holy Scripture, Reformed churches have generally permitted a large degree of freedom in this area. Individual churches were expected to make sure that funeral practices clearly communicated the gospel of salvation by grace, the sure hope of the resurrection, and the consolation of God, but no further prescriptions were made. In fact, no developed liturgies of prayers, readings, or committal ceremonies are found in the Reformed tradition until the nineteenth century, three hundred years after the Reformation.

The Reformed tradition for the burial of the dead, therefore, can be summarized as follows:

A. freedom in the practices or ceremonies to be used;

B. a deep concern that all practices be faithful to the gospel and that they avoid all superstition;

C. an emerging consensus that funerals are religious practices of families rather than official ecclesiastical services;

D. a conviction that the purpose of funerals is the consolation and edification of the living, not the honoring of the dead.

Funerals in the CRC

Until 1940 the Church Order of the Christian Reformed Church read, "Funeral sermons or funeral services shall not be introduced." However, the church's practice was quite different. Funeral services *were* held, at first in the home of the deceased or in the church, and later in funeral chapels. The services were simple: Scripture, meditation, and prayers. The singing of psalms or hymns, although an important part of worship services, was uncommon in funerals until late in the twentieth century. The committal service usually included scriptural sentences, the committal, and a prayer.

In 1940 the Church Order was changed to read, "Funerals are not ecclesiastical, but family affairs, and should be conducted accordingly." This change recognized what had long been the practice of the church: pastors usually consulted with the family, and together they planned the service. Even when funerals were no longer held in the home, the family often had a short service together before taking the casket from the home to the church or chapel for the funeral.

Today, although the funeral service is significant for the grieving family, equally important are the visits of consolation and comfort by friends, neighbors, and extended family. People come to the home of the deceased bearing food, flowers, and compassion. These visits bracket the service and cast the whole occasion as an event of the believing family and the family of God.

In this respect, current customs show a striking resemblance to those of the early church, despite obvious differences in liturgical detail (notably the elimination of the Lord's Supper). The evidence of continuity is interesting from a purely historical standpoint; it should be of equal interest in reflecting on our practices in the future.

Pastoral Care at the Time of Death

A death in the congregation, while never a welcome event in our lives or schedules as pastors and elders, offers important opportunities for ministry. Death pierces through the veil of everyday life and places people face to face with its awesome and inescapable reality. Normal living stops in its tracks for a few days. Families are drawn together, sometimes in ways they have never been together before. Memories are stimulated—some beautiful, some painful. The foundational truths of the Christian faith are talked about, proclaimed, and sometimes even called into question by people who have been rubbed raw by grief.

Such vulnerability creates an atmosphere in which people powerfully experience the care or the callousness of the Christian community. Seldom does the church's pastoral care have as deep an impact on people's lives as at the time of a death. We need to remember this because, especially in larger churches, we may fall into set patterns of ministry, forgetting the unique importance of each death to the family and the individuals involved.

When someone dies, we often unthinkingly follow certain patterns and traditions for funerals and pastoral care without examining *what* we do and *why*. Part of the problem is that few church councils discuss funeral practices and ways of ministering to grieving people—or encourage their congregations to do so. So, often by default rather than by choice, the funeral director who knows the traditions of the church or community guides the family along in their planning.

According to the CRC Church Order, funerals are not ecclesiastical responsibilities; nevertheless, the church's pastoral care and advice is often deeply needed and welcomed at the time of death. The church—not just pastors, but councils and church members as well—should have a well-thought-out framework for what they will do when a death occurs in the church community.

Actually, the need for care often begins before the time of death. More and more frequently today, we face situations in which individuals may linger for days, weeks, or even months at the brink of death. This is a very stressful time for the family, a time in which they desperately need the ministry of the church. As death slowly engulfs the loved one, the awareness of death and the grieving also envelopes the family. Visits during this time are important and fruitful, both for the dying individual and for the family. It is good to visit the dying person alone, to provide opportunity for very personal expressions of faith and doubt, and to offer the consolation of Scripture, prayer, and, perhaps, sacrament. It is also good to visit with the family present in order to listen and participate in their sharing as life ebbs.

After death has occurred, the pastor and other caregivers (such as the elders), need to be notified as soon as possible so that their ministry can surround the grieving. Congregations, too, should be made aware of ways in which they can offer help and support to the bereaved family. (The council or consistory may want to prepare some simple guidelines; see p. 213.)

The most important thing for all caregivers to remember is that in our ministry to grieving people, we represent Christ. Through us, Christ comes to comfort, to listen, to bear burdens, to weep, and to speak of hope. When we minister to grieving people with a deep awareness that we personally represent Christ and depend on him, we will be far more effective.

The following guidelines may help ministers and other comforters to fit their ministry to the realities of grief.

1. Make early, frequent, and brief contacts.

It is important to call on the bereaved as soon as possible after a death has occurred as an immediate sign of the care and love of Christ and his church. The initial visit should probably take no more than half an hour, because the bereaved persons often have much to do and consider, and they sometimes need time alone. Subsequent visits should be made daily, if possible, and should be shorter yet—about fifteen minutes is appropriate. Even a phone contact may be helpful if a visit is not possible or welcomed.

Before making a visit, call ahead and make sure that the family welcomes your presence. If you encounter resistance, you obviously need to honor the family's wishes; we cannot impose our care on people. But keep in mind that such obstinacy may be an important signal of difficulty in the family system, in the family's relationship to the church, or in their coming to terms with grief. In the face of this resistance, however subtle, a listening ear is all the more important.

2. Encourage the grieving to talk about what happened.

We have an almost universal need at the time a loved one dies to talk about exactly what happened. Often people will go into great detail about what they were doing when the phone rang, how they discovered the body, what things looked like and smelled like, and other sometimes grisly details of how death came. This reliving of the details of death is an important step in making the death more real. It's a step that may have to be repeated a number of times, and the need for such recounting may linger for years. In such a situation, the task of the caregiver is to lend an ear.

3. Encourage talking about the deceased person.

The days and weeks immediately after death has occurred are times in which the family needs to frame a verbal picture of the deceased person. There will be many wonderful memories, stories, anecdotes, and tributes from the unique perspective of family members and close friends. Usually there will also be painful memories of wrongs committed and of the hurt caused by troubled relationships. These also need to be shared. If the memories are slanted toward the troubling ones, the family will likely need help in coming to terms with their grief. Sometimes the intervention of a trained therapist may be important a few months down the road.

4. Remember the children.

It is regrettably common to ignore the children in the bereaved family. Grief and its attendant traditions, such as visiting at the funeral home, are often assumed to be adult activities. Children may help us come to that unwarranted conclusion by seeming to be uninvolved or even resistant.

The fact is that children need to grieve and to face the reality of death just as adults do, so it's important that they share in the rituals of grief. For better or for worse, adults model grief for children. They are quick to pick up even unintended spiritualization of grief ("he or she is happier now"), or the denial of grief (never seeing adults "break down" with grief). Witnessing these responses in adults, children quickly assume that this is the way one *ought* to deal with grief. So in trying to "spare" our children, we may actually be leaving them alone and rudderless in a raging sea of grief.

Younger children will have many direct and honest questions about death. They are often curious about the more physical aspects of death and about the body of the deceased person. They may want to touch the body or even kiss the loved one. Adults should be prepared to interpret the feelings, thoughts, and sensations of death (the urge to weep, the cold skin of the deceased, etc.) to children so they can more easily incorporate these things into their childlike world. Families may need to be gently reminded about the needs of children and grandchildren and should be encouraged to answer their questions and respond to their needs simply and honestly. There is no reason not to.

Fear is an additional burden that children face as a result of death. Younger children may be coming to terms with death's reality for the first time. Older children and young people may face fears about who will now care for them or provide for their needs. Fear oppresses children (and adults, for that matter!) a little less when they know that someone understands what they are going through. So adult caregivers should try to help children and young people talk about their fears. We may not have all the answers to their fears, but we can at least ease their anxiety by sharing these concerns.

Older children and teenagers will often be less direct and more covert in their feelings. Pastors and other adult caregivers need to take the time just to listen to what they are feeling and thinking. Teens should also be encouraged to spend time with their peers during these difficult days. Young people value the presence and sympathy of their peers and, even in their grief, teenagers often need to be assured that they are still part of the group.

5. Encourage the release of feelings.

Grief is pain—deep, cutting, emotional pain. Often the pain is increased by other factors, such as anger, doubt, fear, and loneliness. There is no way to avoid the pain. It must simply be embraced and accepted.

As simple as that sounds, many of us have not learned to do it. We secretly believe we can avoid pain if we keep it at arm's length. Sooner or later, however, the energy it takes to keep the pain away exacts more from us than the pain of grief itself. The task of the caregiver is not to encourage stoicism and a stiff upper lip, nor even to stimulate faith and hope, but rather to facilitate the release of painful feelings of grief. It is good for grieving people to cry. It is normal for them to feel angry or abandoned or fearful. They need to be encouraged to simply feel whatever is there.

We may help a person grieve through careful listening and through helping them identify and articulate their feelings: "In your circumstances many people feel . . ." or "It helps some people to cry or get angry . . ." or "It seems to me that you must feel the need to . . ." or "You must be feeling . . . ." Never should we say, "I know just how you feel," a statement that is more likely to cause anger than bring comfort.

We also encourage grief by modeling it ourselves—by not being afraid to weep or be angry. It is important to note in this context that we should never encourage the use of chemical sedation during the period of grieving unless it appears absolutely necessary. Sedatives only delay the grief, which may, in fact, be more difficult to deal with later.

6. Allow for strategic withdrawal and denial.

There are times when nudging a person to grieve is inappropriate. Each person's psyche has its own timetable for coping with grief, and some people need to withdraw for awhile before dealing openly with the trauma. Denial can, in some cases, be a perfectly healthy way of *gradually* coming to terms with an overwhelming event, such as a sudden or tragic death. The caregiver must learn to read both verbal and nonverbal clues to determine when to intervene and when it might be better to step aside for a time.

7. Offer the ministry of touch.

We must never forget that many of Jesus' healing miracles were accompanied by touch. Touch is essential to healing of any sort, including grief. Don't be afraid to hug the bereaved, to put your arms around them, to hold their hands. Words can be cheap, and never more so than in the face of death or tragedy. Touch speaks in a way that often breaks through to the heart better than our words. The closer our ministry is to the death itself, the more true this is. That initial visit may better begin with mostly hugs and tears rather than lots of words, although certainly the ministry of words should follow the ministry of touch.

Keep in mind, though, that not everyone is equally receptive to touch. Some of those to whom we minister may not know us well enough to welcome touch, or may simply not be comfortable with physical contact. Such hesitancy is usually easy to discern, especially nonverbally, and should be honored. Sometimes the reluctance is signaled by the caregiver him/herself. If we are not comfortable with touch, the bereaved will almost certainly pick up our feelings, and they will not welcome physical contact from us—no matter how much they may need it.

8. Seek to listen to and understand the feelings of the bereaved.

Our first task as comforters is not to speak but to listen—not to provide understanding in the face of death, but to understand the wounds of death's blows in the life of the bereaved. Only by attentive listening and profound understanding do we earn the right to speak the words of comfort and faith.

This listening and understanding may be difficult for two reasons. The bereaved, first of all, may signal us in all sorts of ways to talk rather than to listen. They themselves may mouth pieties and cliches in our presence ("This is the pastor or elder, and this is how I'm supposed to feel"). Most of the time these pieties are a denial or cover-up of real feelings of which the person may be ashamed. But a good listener will not be put off track. Comments such as, "I knew someone in your circumstance who . . ." or even, "When that happened to me, I . . ." may help to open up the channels of communication.

The other difficulty in listening may lie in ourselves. To listen, really *listen,* is to be willing to hear and to try to understand terrible pain, deep heartache, grave doubt, and blazing anger. We may not be ready to bear all this—especially if we have never embraced those feelings ourselves. That's why listening requires much more of us than any amount of talking. Comforting and soothing words, spoken too soon, may actually be our way of reassuring *ourselves* that everything will be all right. It takes great discipline and care to offer a truly listening ear and heart.

9. Encourage the bereaved to face the physical reality of death.

We sometimes encounter the attitude among Christians that the real person is the spiritual soul that has gone to heaven. "The body is just dust," they say, "so get the body out of sight and out of mind as soon as possible." That's a mistake. While everyone who views a body can plainly see that it is no longer a person, it is still the body we associate with the person who died.

In death, Christians honor the body because we honor God's good creation. Viewing of the body should be encouraged, unless certain circumstances make it absolutely impossible. Bereaved people, reluctant as they may sometimes be, need to face death in its cold and stark reality. It is, after all, the last enemy. For the same reason, family and friends of the deceased should be encouraged to go to the graveside for the committal, and even to see the casket lowered into the ground.

Cremation is increasingly common, especially in those areas where land is scarce and costly. Christians need not be hesitant about choosing cremation, since there are no biblical or theological grounds to hinder the practice. Since cremation need not happen immediately upon death, family and friends can still have time to view the body and visit together.

Another factor that sometimes influences decisions we make about funerals and related issues is the donation of body parts to medicine. In such cases there is usually a delay, depending on the body parts involved, but the family is still able to view the body. However, if the entire body is donated, it is moved directly to a medical facility and cannot be viewed. Before choosing this alternative, families should be aware that it may be difficult for at least some family members to come to terms with the reality of the death if they are denied a chance to view the body.

10. Encourage involvement in planning.

It is important that those who are grieving have things to do. The phone calls, the visit to the funeral director, and other necessary details can often function benevolently by allowing a time of activity during which the reality of death slowly seeps into the consciousness. Since death leaves us feeling that we have so little control over our environment, these duties and decisions also give the bereaved some semblance, at least, of control over events.

For that reason it is unwise for the caregiver to take over the plans and make contacts on behalf of the bereaved too readily. However, if you sense that the bereaved person is overwhelmed with the preparations and plans or needs guidance on what steps are to be taken, you can certainly offer some help and advice—without taking over full responsibility.

The pastor should play an important role in working with the family to plan the funeral service. If the pastor is going to effectively minister to the family and friends gathered for the funeral, it is absolutely crucial to spend time with the family, listening to stories and sensing feelings. At the funeral, the liturgist or pastor must give public expression to these thoughts and feelings (with a view, of course, to privacy and confidentiality).

Sometimes much advanced planning has already taken place. In fact, funeral directors have, as of late, found a marked increase in preplanning. There may be times when the deceased has preplanned the funeral in a manner that is not helpful to the bereaved. Pastors need to remember that the funeral is for the living, and if there are aspects of the preplanning that they simply cannot accept, they should feel free to change them.

Some families may be ready and willing to plan the funeral themselves. The pastor or elder may not agree with everything that they choose to include, but such planning is their right, and it is also a very helpful way of dealing with their grief. In many cases, however, the family will need some guidance. It is helpful if the pastor comes to the family with at least a basic outline of the service and the various options the family can consider in planning the service.

The pastor and the council also need to be sensitive to matters of cost. Families may experience subtle pressures to "honor the deceased" by purchasing the most expensive casket or by planning the most elaborate funeral when the money could be far more wisely spent in other ways. Councils can greatly help their congregations by discussing these sensitive issues and by giving some general guidelines regarding stewardship in relation to funerals.

Certainly if the family chooses to include anything that is not traditionally done at funerals in the area, the pastor will need to thoroughly discuss it with them. The funeral, like the wedding, is one of the rituals people are very reluctant to change, and important traditions need to be honored. Changes in funeral practices do not usually come quickly, and care needs to be taken not to offend community sensibilities for the sake of liturgical innovation or correctness. The focus of attention must always be the pastoral care of the grieving family and friends. This focus allows for new ideas and suggestions, but it also cautions against applying too much pressure for change. If change is to be made, it is wise to involve the council and the congregation in the process by open discussion of policies and practices.

11. Mobilize the church to offer help for legitimate needs.

When death occurs in a family, there are often so many matters to attend to, so many visitors to greet, and so much grief to work through, that help in peripheral matters can be greatly appreciated. One of the helps the church can best provide is meals for the bereaved family. It is usually best not to ask *whether* meals are needed but rather *when* is the best time to bring them over and for how many people. Other immediate needs the church family can attend to include child care, financial or legal aid, travel arrangements, and a post-funeral luncheon or other get-together. The pastor and council should prepare for these opportunities through proper planning and mobilization of resources.

12. Remember that grieving takes time.

The few days leading up to the funeral are only the very first steps in a rather long journey of grief. Surprisingly to some, these are often the easiest steps. Usually the darkest moments, the greatest loneliness, the deepest stabs of pain come months and even years later. While a sense of loss never ends, the healing process for grief usually takes two or three years. It is helpful for bereaved people to know that, especially so they can resist the often-implied suggestion that they "ought to be over it by now."

The bereaved may also need to be encouraged to continue to explore their feelings in the weeks, months, and years to come. Gentle but probing questions may help this process: "There must be many moments when you still miss ___________" or "I've been thinking about _________; maybe we could share some memories." Unfortunately, while caregivers may understand the length of this process intellectually, it is difficult to maintain significant contact with bereaved persons over such a long stretch. It is important, therefore, that a church council work out practical ways in which their ministry to the bereaved can continue after the funeral. Certainly regular visits need to be made, and cards or calls on the anniversary of a death are also appreciated.

13. Establish a careful, loving, and informed ministry.

While actual practice may differ from community to community, there is always some form of visitation for the bereaved family. Because these hours may seem overwhelming to the family, they sometimes seek to cut down on the time for visitation or avoid it altogether. Pastors and caregivers should help such families understand that although times of visitation are demanding and tiring, this process is important in working through their grief. Through the ritual of visitation, family and friends share their grief in a personal way, relive the death, remember the deceased loved one, comfort one another, and tell those important family stories again and again. Yes, the wounds are reopened over and over, but this is precisely what is necessary in order to grieve in a way that leads back to life.

An often overlooked final step in the funeral is the gathering of family and friends for a meal. This too is a ritual act, affirming that life goes on after death. It functions as a bridge between the highly charged emotions and special activities of the preceding few days and the everyday life to which they must all return. The pastor should not overlook this opportunity to continue in ministry to grieving family and friends.

The ministry to the bereaved cannot only be borne by the officebearers of the church. It is a congregational ministry. Therefore it is very important that the entire congregation be aware of the reality and importance of grief in its many stages and forms. This awareness can be nurtured in a number of ways, from sermon illustrations to a series of adult education classes on grief. In communities that have a Hospice program, any members who have gone through that training and have worked with dying people may be an invaluable resource.

A careful, loving, and informed ministry to bereaved people is certainly one of the most important ministries in the life of the church. It can be carried out properly and consistently only when the entire congregation—not only the leaders but also the members—plan for it, understand its dynamics, and carry it out with loving care.

PRAYERS AND READINGS

Prayers and Readings with Those near Death

The prayers and readings on these pages may be useful for pastors and others who make regular visits to the bedside of a dying person. They are appropriate for a variety of circumstances and situations, and can be used either individually or as part of a structured service. While this ministry should not be done in a liturgically formal manner, it is appropriate and often appreciated that the time before death be marked by a solemnization of the moment. The purpose is to build the faith of the dying person and the family, if they are present, and to prepare them for death.

A structured service of prayer and readings for use when death is near is probably unfamiliar to most people in the modern Reformed tradition, though it is used in many others. The Puritans of the sixteenth century and the *Hervormed Kerken* (Reformed Churches) of the Netherlands, for example, had several such forms for common use. Such a service can be a valuable resource of faith and strength for the dying person and his or her family. But, since it may be unfamiliar, the pastor or other representative of the church should talk with the family beforehand about its use and appropriateness.

Each death, from the gentle passing away of an aged person after a long decline or illness, to the emergency call after an accident or sudden illness, includes its own set of circumstances. So the setting for this service may be a home, a hospital, or even the scene of an accident. The pastor will need to be sensitive to the needs and limitations of the moment. In some cases, the service here may be used directly from the book. In other cases, it may be more appropriate that the prayers be memorized or their themes expressed in one's own words.

The condition of the dying person may also be an important consideration. These prayers and readings are appropriate whether the dying person is conscious or unconscious, and whether or not family or friends are present. Experts and our own experience tell us that we can never be sure how much of our words actually penetrate into the consciousness of a comatose person. So we should always assume that the dying are conscious, appearances to the contrary. One could properly offer these readings and prayers at the bedside of a comatose individual with no one else present.

Physical contact is often very important to the sick and dying. Holding the hand of the dying person, for example, can be a very meaningful gesture of support and human solidarity.

The Service

When these readings and prayers are used as a structured service, the biblical *greeting* alerts all present that the service is beginning. These familiar words, often heard at the beginning of worship, also serve to remind the dying person of his or her place in the body of Christ.

The *opening prayer* focuses attention on baptism, which should function as a handle of faith for the dying person. The Lord's Prayer, so familiar from throughout the life of a believer, can also serve to bolster faith and bring the dying person actively into the prayers, if possible.

The *readings* should be short (use no more than two). This is not a time to wander into unfamiliar texts of Scripture. These are moments when Christians want and need to hear the familiar old words that are easy to spiritually digest and that bring comfort. Perhaps the dying person will request a certain passage.

The *prayers* at this point in the service are of two different types. The earlier prayers are more general petitions for the grace of God in death. The later ones specifically commend the dying person to God's loving and saving care.

Also included in this service is a *commendation*, with the laying of hands upon the head of the dying person. This is not a prayer, but a gesture of farewell and loving commendation on the part of the pastor and all others present. It functions in the same way that a laying on of hands may function in a healing service. Not only the pastor but also family members may lay hands on the head of the dying person, or they may hold hands together around the room. Through this act we are commending the dying person to God for ultimate healing grace.

Attention is then directed again to God with a final *prayer of commendation.* You will notice that this prayer is the same one recommended as the commendation for the funeral service. There is no problem with using the same prayer meaningfully in both cases.

It may be helpful if the *family and friends* present are invited to briefly offer their own words of prayer and commendation. They should be made aware of this opportunity before the service begins. This may be a wonderful opportunity for the loved ones to give expression to their love, their grief, and their faith. However, in the interests of the dying person, the officiant should remain in control of the service lest it wander away from its intent or become too long.

The service is then closed with a *blessing*, accompanied by an appropriate gesture.

If death has already occurred before the pastor arrives, the prayers may begin with the commendation on page 46, and follow with prayers for the bereaved, concluding with the blessing.

The Greeting

The grace of the Lord Jesus Christ,
the love of God the Father,
and the fellowship of the Holy Spirit
be with all of you.
AMEN.

Opening Prayer

Gracious God, look upon _________,
whom you claimed as your own in baptism.
Comfort and strengthen him/her with the promise of
eternal life,
made sure through the resurrection of your Son,
Jesus Christ our Lord.
AMEN.

Let us pray together the prayer that our Lord taught us:

Our Father who art in heaven,
hallowed be thy name;
thy kingdom come;
thy will be done on earth as it is in heaven.
Give us this day our daily bread;
and forgive us our debts, as we forgive our debtors;
and lead us not into temptation, but deliver us from evil.
For thine is the kingdom, and the power,
and the glory, for ever. Amen.
—*KJV*

[or]

Our Father in heaven,
hallowed be your name,
your kingdom come,
your will be done
on earth as it is in heaven.

Give us today our daily bread.
Forgive us our debts,
as we also have forgiven our debtors.
And lead us not into temptation,
but deliver us from the evil one.
For yours is the kingdom and the power
and the glory forever. Amen.
—NIV

Scripture Reading

[One or two passages from Scripture are read. The reading or readings should be kept very brief.]

I have set the LORD always before me.
Because he is at my right hand,
I will not be shaken.

Therefore my heart is glad, and my tongue rejoices;
my body also will rest secure,
because you will not abandon me to the grave,
nor will you let your Holy One see decay.
You have made known to me the path of life;
you will fill me with joy in your presence,
with eternal pleasures at your right hand.
—Psalm 16:8-11

The LORD is my shepherd, I shall not be in want.
He makes me lie down in green pastures,
he leads me beside quiet waters,
he restores my soul.
He guides me in paths of righteousness
for his name's sake.
Even though I walk
through the valley of the shadow of death,
I will fear no evil,
for you are with me;

your rod and your staff,
  they comfort me.
You prepare a table before me
  in the presence of my enemies.
You anoint my head with oil;
  my cup overflows.
Surely goodness and love will follow me
  all the days of my life;
and I will dwell in the house of the LORD
  forever.

—Psalm 23

[Note: For pastoral reasons, reading an older translation of Psalm 23 may be appropriate.]

Praise the LORD, O my soul;
  all my inmost being, praise his holy name.

The LORD is compassionate and gracious,
  slow to anger, abounding in love.

He does not treat us as our sins deserve
  or repay us according to our iniquities.
For as high as the heavens are above the earth,
  so great is his love for those who fear him;
as far as the east is from the west,
  so far has he removed our transgressions from us.
As a father has compassion on his children,
  so the LORD has compassion on those who fear him;
for he knows how we are formed,
  he remembers that we are dust.
But from everlasting to everlasting
  the LORD's love is with those who fear him,
  and his righteousness with their children's children.

—Psalm 103:1, 8, 10-14, 17

When they came to the place called the Skull,
there they crucified him, along with the criminals—
one on his right, the other on his left.
One of the criminals who hung there hurled insults at him:
"Aren't you the Christ? Save yourself and us!"
But the other criminal rebuked him.
"Don't you fear God," he said,
"since you are under the same sentence?
We are punished justly,
for we are getting what our deeds deserve.
But this man has done nothing wrong."
Then he said, "Jesus, remember me when you come
into your kingdom."
Jesus answered him, "I tell you the truth,
today you will be with me in paradise."

—Luke 23:33, 39-43

Jesus said to her, "I am the resurrection and the life.
He who believes in me will live, even though he dies;
and whoever lives and believes in me will never die.
Do you believe this?"
"Yes, Lord," she told him, "I believe that you are the Christ,
the Son of God, who was to come into the world."

—John 11:25-27

Do not let your hearts be troubled.
Trust in God; trust also in me.
In my Father's house are many rooms;
if it were not so, I would have told you.
I am going there to prepare a place for you.
And if I go and prepare a place for you, I will come back
and take you to be with me
that you also may be where I am.

—John 14:1-3

Who shall separate us from the love of Christ?
Shall trouble or hardship or persecution,
or famine or nakedness or danger or sword?
No, in all these things we are more than conquerors
through him who loved us.
For I am convinced that neither death nor life
neither angels nor demons,
neither the present nor the future, nor any powers,
neither height nor depth,
nor anything else in all creation,
will be able to separate us from the love of God
that is in Christ Jesus our Lord.

—Romans 8:35, 37-39

I declare to you, brothers,
that flesh and blood cannot inherit the kingdom of God.
For the perishable must clothe itself with the imperishable,
and the mortal with immortality.
When the perishable has been clothed with the
imperishable
and the mortal with immortality,
then the saying that is written will come true:
"Death has been swallowed up in victory."
"Where, O death, is your victory
Where, O death, is your sting?"
The sting of death is sin, and the power of sin is the law.
But thanks be to God! He gives us the victory
through our Lord Jesus Christ.

—1 Corinthians 15:50, 53-57

Therefore we do not lose heart.
Though outwardly we are wasting away,
yet inwardly we are being renewed day by day.
For our light and momentary troubles
are achieving for us an eternal glory
that far outweighs them all.

So we fix our eyes not on what is seen,
but on what is unseen.
For what is seen is temporary,
but what is unseen is eternal.
Now we know that if the earthly tent we live in is destroyed,
we have a building from God,
an eternal house in heaven, not built with human hands.
—2 Corinthians 4:16-5:1

Then I saw a new heaven and a new earth,
for the first heaven and the first earth had passed away,
and there was no longer any sea.
I saw the Holy City, the new Jerusalem,
coming down out of heaven from God,
prepared as a bride beautifully dressed for her husband.
And I heard a loud voice from the throne saying,
"Now the dwelling of God is with men,
and he will live with them.
They will be his people
and God himself will be with them and be their God.
He will wipe every tear from their eyes.
There will be no more death or mourning or crying or pain,
for the old order of things has passed away."
—Revelation 21:1-4

Prayers

[One of the following prayers is said.]

Gracious God and Father,
you are nearer than our hands and feet,
closer than breathing.
Sustain with your presence our brother/sister __________.
Help him/her now to trust your goodness
and claim your promise of life everlasting.
Cleanse him/her of all sin
and remove all burdens.

Grant him/her the sure joy of your salvation,
through Jesus Christ our Lord.
AMEN.

—*TF*

[or]

Heavenly Father,
we bring before you our brother/sister ________.
In baptism you enfolded him/her with your people;
now bring him/her into your presence
with all the angels and saints in glory.
Even as strength of body ebbs,
may the power of eternal life and peace flood his/her soul.
For we place him/her in your arms, loving Father,
in the faith and hope of ultimate victory,
through Jesus Christ our Lord.
AMEN.

[or]

Almighty God,
by your power Jesus Christ was raised from death.
Watch over our brother/sister ________.
Fill his/her eyes with your light
to see, beyond human sight, a home within your love
where pain is gone
and frail flesh turns to glory.
Banish fear.
Brush tears away.
Let death be gentle as nightfall,
promising a day when songs of joy
shall make us glad to be together with Jesus Christ
who lives in triumph,
the Lord of life eternal.
AMEN.

—*TF*

[or]

Creator God, you made us for yourself;
now take your baptized child, _________, into your loving arms.
Gentle and loving Savior,
you gave up your life on the cross
that we might be redeemed from all our sin;
you rose in victory from the dead
that we might have the promise of eternal life.
Receive into heaven _________, the one you bought with a price.
Holy Comforter,
you are the life of God within us,
drawing us into the circle of heavenly love;
fill _________'s heart with peace and joy
even at the hour of death.
Living God, to whom we belong in life and death,
we commend our brother/sister _________ to your care
in the sure and certain hope of eternal life.
AMEN.

[The following prayer may be used when life-support systems are withdrawn.]

God of compassion and love,
you have breathed into us the breath of life
and have given us the exercise of our minds and wills.
In our frailty we surrender all life to you from whom it came,
trusting in your gracious promises;
through Jesus Christ our Lord.
AMEN.

—*OS*

Commendation

[Then the minister will lay a hand on the head of the dying person, giving other loved ones the opportunity to do the same. The minister will then say:]

Depart in peace, __________, O brother/sister;
In the name of God the Father who created you;
in the name of Christ who redeemed you;
In the name of the Holy Spirit who sanctifies you.
May you rest in peace,
and dwell forever with the Lord.
AMEN.

—BCP

[or]

__________, our brother/sister in faith,
we entrust you to the God who created you;
may you return to the one who formed you
out of the dust of the earth.
We entrust you to Christ who redeemed you;
may that Good Shepherd enfold you in his arms.
We entrust you to the Spirit who sanctified you;
may you shine with all the saints in glory.
May you see your God, face to face,
and enjoy the light of his grace forever.
AMEN.

Prayer of Commendation

Into your hands, O merciful Savior,
we commend your servant __________.
Acknowledge, we humbly pray,
a sheep of your own fold,
a lamb of your own flock,
a sinner of your own redeeming.

Receive him/her into the arms of your mercy,
into the blessed rest of everlasting peace,
and into the glorious company of the saints in light.
AMEN.

—BCP

[or]

O Lord, support us all the days
of this troubled life,
until the shadows lengthen,
and the evening comes,
and the busy world is hushed,
and the fever of life is over,
and our work is done.
Then in your mercy grant us
a safe lodging and a holy rest,
and peace at last;
through Jesus Christ our Lord.
AMEN.

—traditional

Additional Prayers

[One of the following prayers may be said for the family and friends of the dying. Those who are present may also be invited to offer their own prayers.]

Lord God,
look kindly upon us in our sorrow
for this life being taken from us,
and gather our pain into your peace.
Heal our memories,
be present in our grieving,
and overcome all our doubts.
Awaken our gratitude for your gifts of love and tenderness.

As we are able to receive them,
teach us the lessons of life that can be learned in death.
We pray through Christ our Lord.
AMEN.

—*TF*

[or]

Heavenly Father,
even as we commend __________, our beloved, to your care,
we already feel the grief of his/her absence.
We know that he/she will be with you always,
but our sorrow is that he/she will not be with us.
May we find, O Lord, your healing for that pain.
May we come to know that whoever is in you
is always one with us in the body of Christ,
though death may separate us for a time.
Create in us a deeper hope and constant expectation
of that day when we shall all be one again
in the glory of your kingdom, forever.
AMEN.

[or]

Lord Jesus,
our saddened hearts wait for your comfort and peace.
We do not accept death easily,
and we are reluctant to surrender this loved one and friend
to the place you have prepared for him/her.
You know our sorrow, O Lord,
you understand our tears;
for you also wept at the death of a friend.
Let the Holy Spirit, the Comforter you promise,
testify in our hearts to your loving presence.

Be our constant companion, Lord,
as we live through the painful days ahead,
so that, even as we mourn,
we may give witness to our living faith in you.
Through Jesus Christ our Lord.
AMEN.

—UCA

Blessing

[The words of blessing may be offered as a prayer by changing the pronouns to first person plural (i.e.: "The Lord bless us . . .").]

The LORD bless you and keep you;
the LORD make his face shine upon you
and be gracious to you;
the LORD turn his face toward you
and give you peace.
AMEN.

—Numbers 6:24-26

[or]

Go in peace, brother/sister,
and may the blessing of Almighty God,
Father, Son, and Holy Spirit,
be with you now, and in the hour of your death.
AMEN.

Prayers and Readings When Death Occurs

These prayers and readings can be adapted and used for a number of different circumstances after death has occurred and before the funeral service. They may be used informally among a gathering of family and friends in a home. They may also be used when the family first comes to view the body at the funeral home or at an appropriate time during visitation by family and friends of the deceased (such as the vigil, or "wake," a tradition common among Catholic and African-American communities). If the occasion is more formal, a printed order may be used, incorporating some of the prayers and readings from the funeral services or the Additional Resources in this manual.

The Service

When the service takes place in a more formal setting, the biblical words of *greeting* may be used, clearly marking the beginning of the service for all present. Speaking these familiar words, so often used to begin congregational worship, serves to bring the people into a setting of worship.

The use of a *hymn or song* will involve consultation with the family and friends beforehand. Many songs and hymns are familiar enough to the average churchgoing Christian that at least a verse or two can be sung from memory. Hymns such as "Amazing Grace," "Swing Low, Sweet Chariot," or "Beautiful Savior" easily come to mind. Of course, the pastor should have the words clearly in mind and arrange with someone ahead of time to start the song on the correct pitch. In the case of a more formal setting, a hymnbook or printed copies of a hymn or song can be made available.

The *sentences from Scripture* and *call to prayer* offer scriptural permission to grieve before God and call the assembled people to prayer.

Choose the *opening prayer* that best expresses the circumstances of the grieving people you are ministering to. Remember that it is important that the feelings of the bereaved be given expression by the one leading the prayers. Some prayers express a faithful serenity one might imagine at the death of an elderly saint; some express shock and grief at an untimely or tragic death. Again, the prayers are not intended necessarily to be read, though it is not wrong to do so. But they must serve as a *personal* expression that represents the thoughts and feelings of those present. It is therefore important to use the names of the mourners and the one who is being mourned, and to be ready to express what you know of their feelings at this time. If suitable, it can be very meaningful to join hands during the prayer. (Other prayers may be found in the funeral services themselves or in Additional Resources on p. 194ff.) The prayer may be concluded with the Lord's Prayer, for its familiar and ever-meaningful words will bring all those present directly into the spirit of prayer.

A *psalm and other Scripture* may be read. You might use the psalm to give expression to the feelings of grief and loss experienced by the bereaved and the other Scripture to point to the hope we have through the resurrection of Jesus Christ.

This may be a good opportunity for a few brief *remarks from the pastor*, expressing the grief and hope appropriate to the situation, but also calling to mind the life of the deceased person. It can also be very meaningful to invite the *family and friends* gathered together to offer their own *remembrances* and words of faith and hope.

The *prayers* not only express the sadness and hope of the bereaved, but also offer an opportunity to give thanksgiving for the specific gifts and graces that were given by God through the life of the deceased loved one. The specificity of these words may be difficult for the pastor or officiant, but such remembrances in prayer are extremely important for the mourners. Some consultation with the family will greatly help in filling out a verbal portrait of the loved one.

A *commendation* may be included, especially if it has not been used with the family at an earlier time, such as before the death. (See section on prayers for the dead in the commentary on Funeral Service I, p. 78.) In a more formal setting, when a printed order is used, all present may say the words of commendation.

The service will close with a *blessing*, accompanied by an appropriate gesture. The pastor should not leave immediately after prayer; the thoughts and feelings elicited in the prayers may demand the minister's presence a little longer.

Greeting

Leader: The Lord be with you.

People: And also with you.

[or]

The grace and peace of God our Father
and the Lord Jesus Christ be with you.

[or]

The grace and peace of God our Father
who raised our Lord Jesus Christ from the dead,
be with you all.

[or]

May the Father of mercies
and the God of all consolation be with you.

[or]

In this moment of sorrow
the Lord is in our midst
and consoles us with his word:
"Blessed are those who mourn;
for they will be comforted."

—Matthew 5:4

[or]

The eternal God is your refuge,
and underneath are the everlasting arms.

—Deuteronomy 33:27

Hymn or Song

[If a hymnal is not available, select a hymn that is familiar to most people present. The hymn text may be read rather than sung. (See pp. 210-212 for a listing of appropriate hymns.)]

Sentences from Scripture

[One or more of the following verses may be used.]

God is our refuge and strength,
an ever-present help in trouble.

—Psalm 46:1

Blessed are those who mourn,
for they will be comforted.

—Matthew 5:4

When Jesus saw her weeping,
and the Jews who had come along with her also weeping,
he was deeply moved in spirit and troubled.
"Where have you laid him?" he asked.

—John 11:33-34

Call to Prayer

My brothers and sisters, we believe that all the ties of family, friendship and affection which knit us together throughout our lives do not unravel in death. Confident of God's love even in the face of death, let us pray.

—OCF

Opening Prayer

[One or more of the following prayers may be said.]

Our Lord and our God,
the death of our brother/sister __________
reminds us of our frail human condition
and the brevity of our lives on the earth.
Yet for those who are in the embrace of your love
in Jesus Christ our Lord,
death is not the end,
nor can it destroy the bonds
that bind us to you and to each other.
Help us to share that faith together
even through our tears and sadness.
Bring the light of Christ's resurrection
to shine on this time of grief and pain,
through Jesus Christ our Lord.
AMEN.

—OCF

Faithful God, in your wisdom
you have called your servant __________
out of this world.
Though our hearts are heavy with grief,
we willingly place him/her in your loving arms.
Released from the bonds of sin and death,
the old order is passed.

May he/she now receive a glorious welcome
into your heavenly kingdom
where there is no sorrow, no weeping, no pain.
We surrender him/her to your arms
where there is fullness of eternal joy and peace
with your Son, and with the Holy Spirit,
and with all the saints in glory, forever and ever.
AMEN.

Loving God, faithful friend,
our minds and hearts have hardly grasped
what reality demands we accept.
Our dear brother/sister/friend *(etc.)*
is gone from us.
Send us your grace and comfort, O God,
even through the shock and pain.
Assure us again that in your love,
through Jesus Christ our Lord,
not one of your children is ever lost,
but all of us, in life and in death,
are members of your family.
In the darkness and sorrow of this hour
may hope begin to dawn—
hope that points the way to eternal life
beyond the agony of death;
hope that is firm and sure
in the resurrection of Jesus Christ, your Son,
in whose name we pray.
AMEN.

Psalm or Other Scripture

[A Psalm may be sung or read, along with a reading of another brief passage(s) of Scripture. Psalms 16, 23, 27, 46, 91, 103, 121, and 146 may be suitable, either read from Scripture (see pp. 141ff) or as versified in the Psalter Hymnal.

The minister may wish to comment briefly on the passage(s) read and on the life of the deceased. Informal conversation with the family may follow, and those present may be invited to offer their remembrances.]

Prayer

[One or more of the following prayers may be said. (Other prayers may be found on pp. 194ff.)]

Gracious and eternal God,
Lord of life and death,
you made us in your image
and hold us in your care.
We thank you for your servant, __________,
and for the gift of his/her life among us.
We thank you especially for . . .

[Here some of the gifts, work, and qualities of the life of the deceased may be expressed.]

But most of all we thank you for your love in Jesus Christ,
who died and rose again from the grave,
giving us eternal life.
Loving God, when our time on earth is ended,
may we too be united with all the saints
in the joys of your eternal home,
through and with Jesus Christ our Lord.
AMEN.

—TF

Father of mercies and God of all consolation,
you are our refuge in times of trouble,
our light in the darkness,
and our only hope in the valley of the shadow of death.
Comfort your family in their loss and sorrow.
Lift us from the depths of grief
into the peace and light of your presence.

Your Son, our Lord Jesus Christ,
by dying has destroyed our death,
and by rising, restored our life.
Enable us now to press on toward him,
so that, after our earthly course is run,
you may reunite us with those we love,
when every tear is wiped away.
We ask this through Jesus Christ our Lord.
AMEN.

—OCF

Lord God,
you are attentive to the voice of our pleading.
Let us find in your Son
comfort in our sadness,
certainty in our doubt,
and courage to live through this hour.
Make our faith strong,
through Christ our Lord.
AMEN.

—OCF

Lord Jesus, our saddened hearts wait for your comfort and peace.
We do not accept death easily,
and we are reluctant to surrender this loved one and friend
to what seems the cold hand of death.
Gently teach our grieving minds and hearts
that we surrender him/her into your arms.
You know our sorrow, Lord,
and you understand our tears;
for you also wept at the death of your friend.
Let the Holy Spirit, the Comforter you promise,
testify in our hearts of your loving presence.

Be our constant companion, Lord,
as we live through the difficult days ahead,
so that, even as we mourn,
we may give witness to our living faith in you.
Through Jesus Christ our Lord,
AMEN.

—*UCA*

[At the death of a child]

Loving God,
your beloved Son took children into his arms and blessed them.
Give us grace, we pray,
that we may entrust __________ to your never-failing care and love,
and bring us all to your heavenly kingdom;
through Jesus Christ our Lord.
AMEN.

—*LBW*

Commendation

[One or more of the following commendations may be included if not prayed with the family at an earlier time.]

We commend __________, your servant
(or, our brother/sister/friend/parent, etc.)
to you, O Lord who gave him/her life.
May he/she hear your words of welcome,
"Come you blessed of my Father"
and receive the unfading crown of glory.
May the angels surround him/her
and the saints welcome him/her in peace.

[The minister and/or all assembled may say:]

Into your hands, O Lord,
we commend our brother/sister _________.
Gracious God,
in whose presence live all who die in the Lord,
receive our brother/sister _________,
into your merciful arms
and into the joys of your eternal home
with all the departed who rest in your peace.
AMEN.

—*TF*

[These prayers may be concluded with the Lord's Prayer in unison.]

Our Father who art in heaven,
hallowed be thy name;
thy kingdom come;
thy will be done on earth as it is in heaven.
Give us this day our daily bread;
and forgive us our debts, as we forgive our debtors;
and lead us not into temptation, but deliver us from evil.
For thine is the kingdom, and the power,
and the glory, for ever. Amen.

—*KJV*

[or]

Our Father in heaven,
hallowed be your name,
your kingdom come,
your will be done
    on earth as it is in heaven.
Give us today our daily bread.
Forgive us our debts,
    as we also have forgiven our debtors.

And lead us not into temptation,
but deliver us from the evil one.
For yours is the kingdom and the power
and the glory forever. Amen.

—NIV

The Blessing

[The leader closes with one or more of the following blessings. (The words of blessing may be offered as a prayer by changing the pronouns to first person plural: "The Lord bless us . . . .")]

The Lord bless you
and defend you from all evil
and bring you to everlasting life.
AMEN.

—TF

May our almighty and merciful God
bless you and comfort you
and gently wipe away your tears:
in the name of the Father, and of the Son, and of the Holy Spirit.
AMEN.

May the peace of God
which is beyond understanding,
keep your hearts and minds
in the knowledge and love of God
and of his Son, our Lord Jesus Christ.
AMEN.

—Philippians 4:7

Service of Prayer on the Occasion of a Miscarriage, Stillborn Child, or Early Death

A miscarriage or stillborn child is an occasion of deep and painful grief for the family, a grief that can sometimes be overlooked by others and by the church. In such situations, when a funeral service does not seem appropriate, it may be very helpful for the grieving family, along with close relatives and friends, to gather for a brief service of prayer and mutual comfort. Since most families grieve privately in these situations, it may be necessary for the church to make the congregation aware of the availability of this ministry. Certainly, it will be appropriate for the pastor to suggest this service when learning of such a situation in the congregation.

Since this type of service will probably be a new experience for the family, the pastor should explain the intent and the structure of the service beforehand. Probably the most suitable place for the service will be at the graveside, when the baby is interred, or in the intimate setting of the home.

The Service

The pastor or other representative of the church may begin with opening *words of Scripture* and/or *words of invitation.* These words of Scripture and invitation explain the purpose and meaning of this service for the participants. It is important especially to include the words of invitation beginning with "Friends, we have gathered . . . ."

The suggested *prayers* are very direct and honest. Part of the purpose of this service is to give expression to the real feelings of family and friends. It is important to speak to them beforehand to gauge the range and intensity of their feelings. No two situations or families are ever quite alike.

The pastor may wish to give a brief meditation based on Scripture that is evocative of the realities of the situation. Again, it is very important to take seriously the reality of the grief that people feel in these situations and not to look forward too easily to the possibility of another child. *This child* was expected, already loved, and is now gone.

The pastor may, in addition to or in place of the meditation, invite those present to share their feelings along with their hope and faith. This may also be a time for *words of mutual encouragement* offered with appropriate gestures of love and support. Those gathered should be aware of this opportunity before the service begins.

The service closes with a *prayer* and a *benediction.*

Opening Words of Scripture

As a father has compassion on his children,
so the LORD has compassion on those who fear him;
for he knows how we are formed,
he remembers that we are dust.
But from everlasting to everlasting
the LORD's love is with those who fear him,
and his righteousness with their children's children.
—Psalm 103:13, 14, 17

[or]

This is what the LORD says:
"A voice is heard in Ramah,
mourning and great weeping.
Rachel weeping for her children,
and refusing to be comforted,
because her children are no more."
—Jeremiah 31:15

Words of Invitation

Friends, we have gathered here to worship God
and witness to our faith
even as we mourn the death of this infant,
the child of __________ and __________.
We come together in grief, acknowledging our human loss.
May God search our hearts,
that in our pain, we may find comfort;
in our sorrow, we may find hope;
and in death, the promise of the resurrection.

[or]

Jesus said, "Let the little children come to me,
and do not hinder them;
for the kingdom of God belongs to such as these."
—Mark 10:14

[or]

Praise be to the God and Father of our Lord Jesus Christ,
the Father of compassion and the God of all comfort,
who comforts us in all our troubles,
so that we can comfort those in any trouble
with the comfort we ourselves have received from God.
—2 Corinthians 1:3-4

Prayer

All-knowing and ever-loving God,
who remembers even the sparrow when it falls;
though no one else may fully understand
or share our grief at this loss,
you share all our griefs and sorrows;
you know all our broken dreams.
You call us to cast our burdens on you
and in your presence to find comfort.

In this uncertain world, where our dreams fail
and our mortal flesh turns to dust,
grant us grace to taste your eternal love;
through Jesus Christ our Lord.
AMEN.

[or]

Lord, we do not understand why this little one
which we had hoped to bring into the world
has died before birth
(or, has died so shortly after birth).
We only know that where once was sweet expectation,
now there is bitter disappointment;
where once there was hope and excitement,
now there is a feeling of failure and loss.
Nothing can replace this life, this child,
whom we have loved before seeing,
before feeling it stir in the womb.
In our pain we look to you, Lord,
to whom no life is meaningless,
no matter how brief or small.
Though our understanding may be limited,
may it not confine our faith.
Draw us close to you and to each other in our grief.
Heal our wounds and comfort our sorrows,
and raise us all from death to life;
through Jesus Christ our Lord.
AMEN.

[or]

Mysterious Lord of life and death,
a very part of these parents has died
in the death of their child.
Our souls are weighed down with sorrow
and bear a wound whose scar will never leave
all through this life.

Send your Spirit of consolation,
for the pain is heavy and deep.
Come to our aid, Lord of mercy
and Father of our Lord Jesus Christ,
for you saw your Son die on the cross,
and surely you know our pain
at the loss of __________, our beloved child.

Do not take our tears and sorrow as a sign of unbelief,
for we do believe that all of your children who have died
are resurrected to eternal life in you.
Rather, see our tears as a sign of the deep love we felt
 for __________,
who is now gone from us.
As we held him/her in the embrace of our love,
O divine Father, hold him/her close to your heart forever.
Help us, Lord, for we do not seek to understand the why
of this mystery of death so young
as much as we desire to accept it in a holy way,
and to be healed and once again be made whole.
Support us, our Lord and God,
wrap us in your gentle love
as we attempt to carry this bitter burden.
Through Jesus Christ, our Lord.
AMEN.

—PDC

Scripture Readings

[One or two passages of Scripture may be read. Particularly appropriate passages include Isaiah 65:17-25, Zechariah 8:1-8, Matthew 18:1-5 and 10, and Mark 10:13-16 (see pp. 164ff).]

Meditation

[A meditation may be given at this point. If so, it should be quite brief and informal, addressing very personally the needs and feelings of those present.]

Mutual Witness and Comfort

[In place of or in addition to the meditation, family and friends may be invited to briefly voice their feelings and their Christian witness. Signs of faith, hope, and love may be exchanged. Also, a hymn may be sung, such as "Children of the Heavenly Father" (Psalter Hymnal *440).]*

Closing Prayer

Heavenly Father,
as your Son, Jesus, took children in his arms
and blessed them,
so we commit this child to your loving arms.
May we now continue our earthly journey
in grace and hope,
assured that you care for all, small and great, and
looking to that day when we will gather with all your people
in the unending joy of your kingdom;
through Jesus Christ our Lord,
who taught us to pray, ...

[the Lord's Prayer follows]

Our Father who art in heaven,
hallowed be thy name;
thy kingdom come;
thy will be done on earth as it is in heaven.
Give us this day our daily bread;
and forgive us our debts, as we forgive our debtors;
and lead us not into temptation, but deliver us from evil.
For thine is the kingdom, and the power,
and the glory, for ever. Amen.

—*KJV*

[or]

Our Father in heaven,
hallowed be your name,
your kingdom come,
your will be done
  on earth as it is in heaven.
Give us today our daily bread.
Forgive us our debts,
  as we also have forgiven our debtors.
And lead us not into temptation,
but deliver us from the evil one.
For yours is the kingdom and the power
and the glory forever. Amen.
    —*NIV*

Benediction

[One of the following blessings may be used.]

The peace of God,
which transcends all understanding,
guard your hearts and your minds
in Christ Jesus.
AMEN.

[or]

And the blessing of Almighty God,
Father, Son and Holy Spirit,
stay with you, now and forever.
AMEN.

THE FUNERAL SERVICE

Funeral Service I

Prayers and readings with those who are near death, and with family members after death occurs, take place in a private context—often in a home or a hospital. But a funeral takes on a different tone. At that time the family and close friends need the support of the larger Christian community, and the larger family of believers needs an opportunity to offer comfort and give expression to their own grief and hope.

There is no better way for the Christian community to meet at such a time than in worshiping the God who binds us together as one body in Christ. When one member of the body suffers, all the members suffer, and we respond by turning to the Lord together in worship. Therefore, the funeral services in this resource are services of worship. All the elements of worship will be present (except the offering and the sacrament of Holy Communion): hymns, Scripture, sermon, affirmation of faith, and prayer.

Although these services are called funeral services, they could also serve as memorial services. The same structure is appropriate for both, and families who choose to have both a private funeral and a public memorial service may use the same basic model for both—especially if those services are separated by several hours or even days, and take place in different locations. If the funeral service is held shortly before a memorial service, it may be shorter and more intimately directed toward the family and close friends in attendance. The statement of faith could perhaps be included in the committal or memorial service, and the singing would undoubtedly be richer in the context of the larger community, but otherwise, the same elements of worship should be present for the funeral as for the memorial service. Throughout this commentary, reference to the funeral service could as well be applied to the memorial service.

The focus of the funeral service is to give witness to our faith in the resurrection of Jesus Christ and to our hope of resurrection through him. It can therefore strike a note of deeply felt joy and firm faith. At the same time, the funeral service may provide opportunity for the expression of profound grief and painful questioning. That these two moods can stand side by side in a funeral is a reflection of our honesty in worship before the face of God, and the very nature of our present situation as believers. We are living between the times, and we are "already, but not yet" fully redeemed. Such honest expression of both grief and faith, side by side, before God and others, is an essential part of the grieving process.

It is important, therefore, that the liturgist pay careful attention to whether both soaring faith and painful grief are given proper expression in the funeral service. The balance will, of course, depend somewhat on the situation. Also, it ought to be assumed that the person responsible for the liturgy will pay careful attention beforehand to such details as consultation with the musician(s), setting, orientation of participants, and general mood and flow of the service. The funeral service is a crucially important ministry that the congregation offers to the bereaved, a gift that lingers long in the mind and heart.

While the basic liturgical structure of the service may remain the same, it is important also to personalize the service. A funeral is not a regular Sunday service of worship, but a unique event in the lives of those present. Appropriate words and gestures that personalize the service are often welcome. The most frequent complaint about funerals is that they are too generic. (On planning a service with the family see "Pastoral Care at the Time of Death," p. 21.)

The Place

It is assumed in this commentary that the funeral will be held in the church building or sanctuary. In places where this is not a regular practice, the consistory should discuss the question seriously. Our reluctance to have funerals in the church may go back to the way funerals are dealt with in the Church Order of the Christian Reformed Church—as family matters rather than as ecclesiastical services. The assumption may have been that since the funeral is not an ecclesiastical matter, it should not be held in the church building, where it might look too much like a worship service.

In practice, however, we have sometimes held large funerals for prominent church members in the church building, and small funerals for all others in the funeral chapel. Thus, a subtle discrimination invades our funeral practice. Since the funeral service is a worship service, and since the church building is the spiritual home of our church family—where we are baptized and married, and where we gather weekly for the Word and the sacraments—what more suitable place can there be for a funeral? Sometimes, of course, a very small group may feel out of place in a church and may thus prefer the smaller, more intimate feel of the funeral chapel. But usually inadequate space, poor acoustics, and inferior musical instruments make the funeral chapel far less suitable than the church for the type of worship we intend for a funeral.

The Prelude

The purpose of the musical prelude is to bring the congregation into the spirit of faithful worship. The music should therefore not call attention to itself, but should lead the gathered congregation into God's presence.

Often the prelude is a wonderful time to use the great and familiar hymns of the church in various arrangements. The familiar tunes draw worshipers in and help them think through the well-known, meaningful words that they have sung so often together. The musician should consult with the family so that he or she can include some hymns that the family feels are particularly appropriate.

The prelude may also provide an opportunity for a family member with a musical gift to offer it to God in memory of the deceased loved one. It is important, however, that the church musician evaluate such a contribution ahead of time to ensure that the quality of the musical offering does not detract from the overall spirit of the service, and that the music and lyrics are appropriate for the situation. This is not to say that a musical offering needs to be highly sophisticated in order to be appropriate; a simple hymn or song, sung or played by a family member, can be very effective.

The Coffin

The coffin should always be closed for the funeral so that the people focus on the promises of God rather than on the body of the deceased. If the family desires, arrangements can be made for viewing the body in a vestibule, narthex, or some other suitable part of the church before the service begins.

The Pall

Some congregations are restoring the ancient custom of covering the casket with a pall. A pall—a white cloth usually decorated with symbols of the Christian faith—can be a meaningful addition to a funeral. In baptism, we are clothed with the righteousness of Christ. So the words used in the liturgy for the placing of the pall point directly to baptism as the sign and seal of our death and resurrection with Christ. Through the use of a pall, the congregation is reminded that death (symbolized by the coffin) is transformed by baptism into Christ's death and resurrection—into ultimate victory. The pall visualizes the shared faith of the congregation.

The pall is also a great equalizer. The poor, with their simple cloth-covered coffins, and the rich, with their coffins of polished oak, are equal before God and the eyes of God's people. The only status recognized here is the status of the grace of God in baptism.

Worship committees and consistories should discuss the use of a pall for funerals of members and their families (of course, with the consent of the family in each case). A pall, either made by members of the congregation or purchased at a church supply house, can become a lasting and important reminder of the communion of the saints through baptism into Christ. In those situations where the use of a pall is being introduced, it will be important to educate the congregation as to its meaning.

The Procession

The procession, bringing the coffin to the front of the church, has a long and venerable tradition. Through this ceremony the body of the deceased enters the familiar environment of the church, among the baptized community, for the last time, and leaves commended into God's hands. Generally, the minister(s) and other liturgists lead the procession followed by the pallbearers with the coffin (foot first). The family (if not previously seated) follows at the end of the procession.

The Opening Sentences of Scripture

The liturgist may choose one or two of the suggested scriptural sentences. If a pall is not used, overriding consideration should be given to the sentences from Romans 6 that refer to baptism, since this sacrament points so vividly to the meaning of death for a Christian.

Psalm, Hymn, or Spiritual Song

Singing is a vitally important element in the funeral service, since it gives the congregation an opportunity to express their faith. Obviously the hymns, psalms, or spirituals should be chosen with great care, and, preferably, in consultation with the family of the deceased. Their choices should be honored, if at all possible, but the liturgist should also be sensitive to quality and liturgical appropriateness. Also, the songs that are chosen should be familiar, at least to the worshiping community. A funeral is not a good time to learn new hymns. The opening hymn should be an expression of praise to God or to Christ, focusing on salvation as deliverance from sin and death (see "Music for the Funeral," p. 205).

Prayers

The Call to Prayer provides an opportunity to speak directly to the congregation about the sorrow and the hope with which they have come to the funeral service. It explains the meaning and purpose of the funeral. The prayers throughout this service are offered as models. The liturgist may use them as written, or better, augment them with words chosen to fit the situation more meaningfully. Prayer is certainly one of the most important elements of a funeral service. Its purpose is to give expression to the faith of the people, their thanksgiving to God for the life of the deceased person, and their own groaning grief.

It is important that, whether the prayer is used as written, or is augmented or composed by the liturgist, careful and thoughtful preparation be made. Just as free prayer can, without adequate forethought, become a mere jumble of trite phrases, unconnected with the reality of the situation, so written prayers can be thoughtlessly used without sensitivity to the unique factors of the present situation. The careful liturgist will plan the use of the written prayers and supplement them with deep awareness of the needs and feelings of the people gathered together for the funeral.

One important matter for the children of the Reformation is the issue of praying for the dead. Without going into the whole history of this question, it is clear that there is a strong reticence on the part of Reformed people to pray for the dead. Such prayers can leave one with the mistaken sense that there is a period of purgatorial waiting and testing for the deceased and that somehow our intervention can help determine the person's final lot.

So you may be surprised to find that in some of the prayers, particularly in the Commendation, recommended near the close of the service, we have included what may be construed as prayers for the dead. Certainly, if the liturgist feels uncomfortable with this, these prayers can be easily excluded. But we believe that an important aspect of prayer at the funeral is the giving of the deceased person into the hands of God for merciful care and keeping. We may presume that a baptized person who has professed faith in Jesus Christ is a child of God. Our whole demeanor and attitude at a funeral will be affected by this assumption of grace. Without presuming to make a final judgment, we act and speak on the basis of what we have seen and heard. In that case, may we not commend such a person to God as a "sheep of your own fold, a lamb of your own flock, a sinner of your own redeeming"? (See p. 98.) In appealing to God's mercy in that way, we express what must be our own attitude in facing death, trusting in God's promises and placing ourselves and our eternal destiny into God's loving hands.

This kind of prayer is psychologically important for the bereaved as well. It is a conscious and trusting act of giving the beloved person back into the hands of God from whom he or she has come as a gift, and doing so in the context of faith, hope, and love. Jesus' prayer, "Into your hands I commend my spirit," models this kind of prayer.

The Remembrance

It is often said that the funeral is not for the dead, but for the living. One of the greatest needs of the living, besides the strength and comfort of biblical faith, is to remember the loved one who has died. Certainly this has been the purpose of many of the formal and informal gatherings of family and friends leading up to the funeral, but it also needs to be part of the funeral itself.

This remembering can be done in two ways—either as part of the funeral sermon or as a separate act. However, weaving memories throughout the funeral sermon is often inadequate. Certainly there must always be some interaction between the text as it is preached and the person who has died. But making the sermon the only place in the service where remembrance takes place can tempt the preacher to turn the funeral sermon into a eulogy, only tangentially related to the text.

Often one or two family members or friends can provide a very personal and moving portrait of the deceased loved one far better than the officiant can. In my experience, these have frequently been the most memorable and healing parts of the service. For a very small funeral, it may be appropriate for the officiant to give opportunity for anyone present to offer brief reminiscences.

If you plan to ask someone to do a remembrance, be sure to allow them adequate time to prepare. It may not be wise to have a very close family member take part in this way, especially if the death was tragic or sudden or particularly painful for the family. But most people will be able to give an honest assessment of their ability to perform this task.

It may be helpful to give some guidance to the person giving the remembrance by suggesting the time limits, the need to speak not only of the strengths, but also of some weaknesses of the loved one, the use of humor, and the importance of stories. It is also helpful to suggest to all but the most accomplished speakers that a written manuscript or outline will help them to remember what they want to say and aid them in dealing with the emotions of the moment.

The remembrance is suggested for one of two points in the service, depending on the structure. It may come early, before the Scripture readings, or it may come after the readings, just before the reading of the text for the funeral sermon.

Scripture Readings

The Prayer for Illumination will help to focus the attention of the congregation on the reason for reading Scripture, and will prepare them for more attentive listening.

The readings should be carefully selected to fit the situation of the funeral. There are many beautiful and appropriate passages of Scripture for the funeral, but it is important to keep in mind that grieving people also have a reduced capacity to be attentive for long periods of time. It is recommended, therefore, that the readings be kept short, and that there be only one reading from each of the four categories. It is also strongly recommended that the psalm be either sung, or read in some responsive arrangement. The liturgist should keep in mind that familiar texts often speak more meaningfully than unfamiliar texts because the congregation can more readily understand and integrate them into their overburdened minds and hearts.

The liturgist should not avoid texts that speak of the devastation and agony of death. Such readings may aid the grieving process. A number of these are included throughout this book, especially from the Psalms. To read only positive and hopeful texts will tend to tranquilize the mourners and inhibit their grief and therefore their healing. The Bible is both brutally honest about death's tragedy and hopeful about our ultimate victory over this "last enemy."

It may also be helpful to invite certain family members or friends to read Scripture, particularly those passages that were favorites of the deceased loved one. Again, adequate preparation is important. The reader should be selected carefully (are they capable of reading in this situation?), given the passage well ahead of time, and be given a few tips on reading in public (pace, emphasis, volume, etc.), if necessary. Immediately prior to the sermon the preacher should read the lesson on which the sermon will be based.

The Sermon

The purpose of the funeral sermon is, as with any sermon, the exposition of the Word of God in Scripture to the worshiping community. But a sermon cannot be preached either on Sunday or at a funeral without a thorough interaction with the life situation of the congregation. At a funeral, this life situation is the grief the congregation shares at the death of a loved one and the particular burdens they may carry because of the circumstances of the death. In the case of the death of an elderly person, grief may be less of a focus than a spirit of thanksgiving for that person's life. At any rate, the preacher must diagnose the situation in a very intimate and personal way in order to speak to the heartfelt needs of the gathered congregation.

As mentioned above, making the remembrance a separate part of the service offers the preacher greater freedom to concentrate on the passage and its exposition in the sermon. But even then, the sermon cannot ignore the life of the deceased and the feelings of the congregation. These real-life situations will be woven throughout the proclamation of the Scripture passage.

The preacher will sometimes face extraordinary situations, such as suicide, murder, the death of children or young people, or the presence of factors such as alcoholism, drug addiction, or AIDS. In the face of such tragedies the preacher will agonize over what to say and how much to say. However, there are a couple of factors to keep in mind. It is usually important and even therapeutic to speak openly about the situation. A funeral service should not be a coverup. Without breaking confidentiality or causing undue grief or embarrassment for the loved ones, the preacher must try to address the reality of the situation. For example, the preacher can speak honestly and helpfully about the despair that led to suicide, and the anger mixed in with the grief of the family left behind. There are a number of very helpful books that give guidance to the preacher who faces such situations.

No matter what the situation, the funeral celebrates our hope through the death and resurrection of Jesus Christ. It is not the task of the preacher to decide anyone's eternal destiny. But the sermon must point clearly and unmistakably to Christ as the only one who can save us and give us hope for eternal life. While evangelism should never be the whole focus of the sermon, the preacher must bear in mind that there are likely some people gathered at the funeral for whom this will be a rare opportunity to hear the gospel.

That does not mean that the funeral ought to be turned into an evangelistic service. Too heavy an evangelistic emphasis can tend to make unbelievers feel trapped and offended, and the objective of their hearing the gospel can be lost. But certainly, in looking over the sermon, the preacher must be convinced that anyone who listens to the sermon will be confronted with the good news of victory over sin and death through our Lord Jesus Christ.

Creed or Other Statement of Faith

Grieving people need to give expression to their faith in the familiar words of the creeds and confessions. The Apostle's Creed is included in the funeral service because it is the most commonly known creed of the church, and it gives full expression to the faith. Do not assume that everyone knows the Creed, however. It is important to give page numbers in the hymnal where it can be found or to provide the words in a bulletin or in some other printed form.

Various other suitable scriptural or confessional statements of faith that can be used either here or in the Committal Service are listed in Additional Resources.

Prayers and Commendation

(See pp. 78-79, under Prayers.)

Benediction, Hymn, and Recessional

The benediction is the last word that God speaks to the congregation as they leave to go to the committal or back to their homes. It should be spoken with an appropriate gesture (one or two arms raised over the congregation) while looking at the congregation.

The closing hymn is the last word the congregation speaks to each other and to God in the funeral. While psalms, hymns, or spiritual songs at other points in the service may well express grief and loss, this one should express praise to our saving God and affirmation of our victorious faith through Jesus Christ (see Music for the Funeral, p. 205).

The Prelude

The Placing of the Pall (optional)

[When the pall is placed in the presence of the congregation, the following may be said in addition to or in place of the opening sentences.]

For all of you who were baptized into Christ
have clothed yourselves with Christ (Gal. 3:27).
In his/her baptism, _________ put on Christ;
in the day of Christ's coming,
he/she shall be clothed with Christ's glory.

[or]

All of us who were baptized into Christ Jesus
were baptized into his death.
We were therefore buried with him through baptism into
death
in order that, just as Christ was raised from the dead
through the glory of the Father, we too may live a new life.
If we have been united with him like this in his death,
we will certainly also be united with him in his resurrection.
—*Romans 6:3-5*

[A pall is placed over the coffin.]

Procession

Opening Sentences of Scripture

[One or several of the following sentences from Scripture may be used.]

The psalmist proclaims:

My heart is glad and my tongue rejoices;
  my body also will rest secure,
because you will not abandon me to the grave,
  nor will you let your Holy One see decay.
You have made known to me the path of life;
  you will fill me with joy in your presence,
  with eternal pleasures at your right hand.
  —Psalm 16:9-11

God is our refuge and strength,
  an ever-present help in trouble.
Therefore we will not fear.
  —Psalm 46:1-2

As a father has compassion on his children,
  so the LORD has compassion on those who fear him;
for he knows how we are formed,
  he remembers that we are dust.
  —Psalm 103:13-14

Our help is in the name of the LORD,
  the Maker of heaven and earth.
  —Psalm 124:8

I will praise the LORD all my life.

Blessed is he whose help is the God of Jacob,
  whose hope is in the LORD his God.

The LORD watches over the alien
  and sustains the fatherless and the widow.
  —Psalm 146:2, 5, 9

The LORD says:

As a mother comforts her child,
so will I comfort you.
—Isaiah 66:13

Jesus says:

Blessed are those who mourn,
for they will be comforted.
—Matthew 5:4

Come to me, all you who are weary and burdened,
and I will give you rest.
—Matthew 11:28

Let the little children come to me,
and do not hinder them,
for the kingdom of God belongs to such as these.
—Mark 10:14

I am the resurrection and the life.
He who believes in me will live, even though he dies;
and whoever lives and believes in me will never die.
—John 11:25-26

The apostle Paul writes:

All of us who were baptized into Christ Jesus
were baptized into his death.
We were therefore buried with him through baptism into death
in order that, just as Christ was raised from the dead
through the glory of the Father,
we too may live a new life.
If we have been united with him like this in his death,
we will certainly also be united with him in his resurrection.
—Romans 6:3-5

If we live, we live to the Lord;
and if we die, we die to the Lord.
So, whether we live or die,
we belong to the Lord.

—Romans 14:8

Praise be to the God and Father of our Lord Jesus Christ,
the father of compassion and the God of all comfort,
who comforts us in all our troubles,
so that we can comfort those in any trouble
with the comfort we ourselves have received from God.

—2 Corinthians 1:3-4

We believe that Jesus died and rose again
and so we believe that God will bring with Jesus
those who have fallen asleep in him.
And so we will be with the Lord forever.
Therefore encourage each other with these words.

—1 Thessalonians 4:14, 17, 18

The apostle Peter writes:

Praise be to the God and Father of our Lord Jesus Christ! In his great mercy he has given us new birth into a living hope through the resurrection of Jesus Christ from the dead, and into an inheritance that can never perish, spoil or fade—kept in heaven for you.

—1 Peter 1:3-4

Psalm, Hymn, or Spiritual Song

[congregation standing]

Call to Prayer

Brothers and sisters,
we have come together to renew our trust in Christ
who, by dying on the cross, has freed us from eternal death
and, by rising, has opened for us the gates of heaven.
Let us pray *(or be thankful)* that our brother/sister
may share *(or shares)* in Christ's victory over death,
and let us pray for ourselves,
that the Lord may grant us
the gift of his loving consolation.

—OCF

[or]

Brothers and sisters,
let us now turn our hearts to God in prayer
that he might strengthen our faith,
and grant us his peace and comfort.

[or]

We have gathered here in sorrow and in hope
at the death of __________.
Let us now share our grief with God
and seek his comfort.

Prayer(s)

[One or more of the following prayers may be offered.]

Heavenly Father, our Creator and Redeemer,
in whose presence there is no darkness and no death:
We worship and adore you, the Living God.
Lord Jesus Christ, the Resurrection and the Life,
who tasted death for everyone
and who brought life and immortality to light:
We praise your name for victory over death and the grave.
Holy Spirit, author and giver of life,

Comforter of those who sorrow:
We praise your name for the light and hope
of your presence within our hearts.
Before you, Holy and Triune God,
we offer our worship and adoration,
even in the face of death and the grave:
Blessing and honor,
glory and power,
wisdom and strength,
belong to you, now and forever,
AMEN.

—TF

O God, who brought us to birth,
you are always ready to hear us when we pray.
Even as sorrow pierces our hearts
at the death of __________, our brother/sister,
and we grope for words to express our pain;
you know all our needs before we ask,
and are ready to supply them all
out of the riches of your grace in Jesus Christ.
Show us now that grace,
that as we face the mystery of death,
we may see the light and hope of eternity.
Speak to us once more that solemn message of life and death.
Help us to live as those prepared to die.
And when our days here are ended,
enable us to die as those who go forth to live,
so that, living or dying,
our life may be in Jesus Christ, our risen Lord.
AMEN.

—BS

Eternal God and Father,
gathered around your throne in glory
is that great company of all those who have kept the faith,
finished their race, and now rest from their labors.
We give you praise and thanks
that you have now received __________ into your presence.
Help us here on earth to believe that which we cannot see,
trusting in Christ who said,
"I go to prepare a place for you."
Bring us all at last with all your saints
into the joy of your eternal home,
through Jesus Christ our Lord.
AMEN.

—*BS*

Eternal God, Shepherd of your people,
on this solemn occasion
we feel the fleeting passage of life,
and we know how fragile is our existence
on this tiny planet amid the spinning galaxies.
We confess with the prophet:
"All flesh is grass,
and all its glory is like the flowers of the field.
The grass withers and the flowers fall . . . ."
Yet we also confess:
"the word of our God stands forever."
Teach us to number our days,
that we may gain a heart of wisdom.
We look to you as frightened children look to their mother,
for you alone can comfort us.
Have mercy on us, O God.

See our tears and hear our cries,
and lead us all, as pilgrims,
through this valley of death's shadow
into the light of the resurrection of Jesus Christ
your Son, our Lord.
AMEN.

God of grace and glory,
we remember before you this day
our brother/sister _________.
We thank you for giving him/her to us,
his/her family and friends,
to know and to love as a companion on this earthly pilgrimage.
In your boundless compassion, console us who mourn.
Give us faith to see in death the gateway of eternal life,
so that in quiet confidence
we may continue our course on earth
until, by your call,
we are united with those who have gone before;
through Jesus Christ our Lord.
AMEN.

Most merciful God, whose wisdom is beyond our understanding:
deal graciously with _________ (names) in their grief.
Surround them with your love,
that they may not be overwhelmed by their loss,
but have confidence in your goodness,
and strength to meet the days to come;
through Jesus Christ our Lord.
AMEN.

[At the death of a child]

Loving Father,
you are nearest to us when we need you most.
In this hour of sorrow we turn to you,
knowing that you love us
and trusting in your perfect wisdom.
We thank you for the gift of this child
and for his/her baptism into your church,
for the joy he/she gave all who knew him/her,
for the precious memories that will always abide with us,
and especially for the assurance that he/she lives forever
in the joy and peace of your presence;
through Jesus Christ our Lord.
AMEN.

[Other prayers appropriate to specific circumstances can be found in Additional Resources.]

Remembrance

[A family member(s) or friend(s) may offer a remembrance of the life and gifts of the deceased.]

Prayer for Illumination

[A prayer for illumination may be said before the Scriptures are read. Or the congregation may sing a prayer song, such as "O Word of God Incarnate" (Psalter Hymnal *279).]*

Eternal God,
your love for us is everlasting;
you alone can turn the shadow of death
into the brightness of morning light.
Help us to turn to you now with reverent and believing hearts.
In the stillness of this solemn hour,
speak to us of eternal things,
so that, hearing the promises of Scripture,
we may have hope

and be lifted above the darkness and distress
into the light and peace of your presence,
through Jesus Christ our Lord.
AMEN.

—*TF*

[or]

Lord Jesus Christ,
you are the living Word of God.
To whom else should we go?
For you have the words of eternal life.
As we listen to your Word,
may your Spirit write its message on our hearts
and feed our souls with its nourishing truth.
AMEN.

The Readings

[It is suggested that the Scriptures be read in this order: Old Testament, Psalm, New Testament, and Gospel. Usually no more than one passage should be read from each category. If one of the passages to be read will be the basis for the sermon, it should be read last, with an intervening psalm or hymn between it and the other passages. The interval might also be an appropriate time for the Remembrance.]

Old Testament
Psalm *(read, recited, or sung)*
Epistle
Gospel
[Hymn, Psalm, or Remembrance]
Sermon Lesson

Sermon

[A brief sermon should proclaim the gospel and offer hope and comfort to the bereaved. Especially if there was no Remembrance, memories of the life of the deceased and expressions of gratitude to God for his/her life ought to be included.]

Psalm, Hymn, or Spiritual Song and/or Creed or other Statement of Faith

[A creed or other statement of faith is also suggested in the Committal Service. If the Apostles' Creed is used for the funeral service, select a different statement of faith for the Committal (see pp. 187ff).]

I believe in God, the Father almighty,
creator of heaven and earth.

I believe in Jesus Christ, his only Son, our Lord,
who was conceived by the Holy Spirit
and born of the Virgin Mary.
He suffered under Pontius Pilate,
was crucified, died, and was buried;
he descended to hell.
On the third day he rose again from the dead.
He ascended to heaven,
and is seated at the right hand of God the Father almighty.
From there he will come to judge the living and the dead.

I believe in the Holy Spirit,
the holy catholic church,
the communion of saints,
the forgiveness of sins,
the resurrection of the body,
and the life everlasting. Amen.

—The Apostles' Creed

Prayers

[One or more of the following prayers may be offered.]

God of all grace,
you sent your Son, our Lord Jesus Christ,
to bring life and immortality into the world.
We give you thanks
that by his death he destroyed the grip of death
and that by his resurrection he opened the kingdom of God
to all believers.

Make us confident that because he lives,
we shall also live.
Deepen our conviction that neither death nor life,
nor things present nor things to come,
nor anything else in all creation
shall be able to separate us from your love.
Immerse us now in that love,
which is in Christ Jesus, our Lord
who lives with you and the Holy Spirit,
one God, now and forever.
AMEN.

Living and eternal God,
before whom the generations rise and pass away;
from age to age your people have sought you
and have found that of your faithfulness there is no end.
Our mothers and fathers too have walked their pilgrimage
in the light of your guidance and grace.
Now to us, their children,
be a pillar of fire by night and of cloud by day.
AMEN.

Our heavenly Father,
we give you thanks for __________,
our __________, *(father/mother/brother/sister/friend/loved one)*
who, as a gift of your grace,
entered and so deeply enriched our lives.
We remember your mercies to __________, your servant,
for like us all, he/she needed your forgiveness and grace.
We thank you for all in him/her that was good and kind
and faithful.
We especially thank you for:

[here mention may be made of his/her special gifts and service]

Now may he/she hear your commendation:
"Well done, good and faithful servant,
enter into the joy of your Lord."
AMEN.

God of all grace and comfort,
you heal the broken in heart and bind up their wounds;
look compassionately on us in our grief and loss.
In our sorrow, draw us all closer to you
and to one another as your children.
We especially pray for:

*[here mention may be made of particular loved ones
and special circumstances of grief.]*

Having given us this new tie to bind us to heaven,
grant that where our treasure is,
there may our hearts be also.
Help us to see through the veil of grief
to that glorious day when all shadows will flee,
all mysteries will be revealed,
and all tears wiped away,
through Jesus Christ our Lord.
AMEN.

Heavenly Father,
in Jesus Christ, your Son,
you promised many rooms within your house.
Give us the faith to see
beyond touch and sight, space and time,
a vision of the heavenly city.
And when our vision fails,
help us to trust your loving promises which never fail.
Walk beside us, Lord Jesus,
and help us shoulder the heavy burden of sorrow,
so that we can continue to bravely walk our earthly way.

And may we look forward with glad hearts
to that happy reunion and joyful feast,
when all your people will be gathered into your kingdom
to live with you in peace and joy forever,
through Jesus Christ our Lord.
AMEN.

—TF

Father of mercies and God of all consolation,
you are our refuge in times of trouble,
our light in the darkness,
and our only hope in the valley of the shadow of death.
Comfort your family in their loss and sorrow.
Lift us from the depths of grief
into the peace and light of your presence.
Your Son, our Lord Jesus Christ,
by dying has destroyed our death,
and by rising, restored our life.
Enable us now to press on toward him,
so that, after our earthly course is run,
you may reunite us with those we love,
when every tear is wiped away.
We ask this through Jesus Christ our Lord.
AMEN.

—OCF

Lord Jesus,
our saddened hearts wait for your comfort and peace.
We do not accept death easily,
and we are reluctant to surrender this loved one and friend
to the place you have prepared for him/her.
You know our sorrow, O Lord,
you understand our tears;
for you also wept at the death of a friend.
Let the Holy Spirit, the Comforter you promise,
testify in our hearts to your loving presence.

Be our constant companion, Lord,
as we live through the painful days ahead,
so that, even as we mourn,
we may give witness to our living faith in you.
Through Jesus Christ our Lord.
AMEN.

—UCA

[The Prayer(s) may be closed with a Commendation.]

Commendation

Into your hands, O merciful Savior,
we commend your servant ________.
Acknowledge, we humbly pray,
a sheep of your own fold,
a lamb of your own flock,
a sinner of your own redeeming.
Receive him/her into the arms of your mercy,
into the blessed rest of everlasting peace,
and into the glorious company of the saints in light.
AMEN.

—BCP

[or]

Holy God,
by your creative power
you gave us the gift of life,
and in your redeeming grace
you gave us new life in Jesus Christ.
We commend ________
to your merciful keeping
through faith in Jesus Christ our Lord,
whose death saved us from sin
and whose resurrection brings us eternal life.
AMEN.

—SMT

[or]

Into your hands, Father of all mercies,
we commend our brother/sister _________
in the sure and certain hope
that together with all who have died in Christ,
he/she will rise with him on the last day.
You opened the gates of eternal life to your servant;
now help us who remain to comfort one another
until we all meet again
in the new heavens and the new earth,
through Jesus Christ our Lord,
AMEN.

—OCF

The Lord's Prayer

[When the Lord's Prayer is used at the end of the prayer(s), the prayer(s) will be closed with these words: "through Jesus Christ our Lord, who taught us to pray, saying . . . ."]

Our Father who art in heaven,
hallowed be thy name;
thy kingdom come;
thy will be done on earth as it is in heaven.
Give us this day our daily bread;
and forgive us our debts, as we forgive our debtors;
and lead us not into temptation, but deliver us from evil.
For thine is the kingdom, and the power,
and the glory, for ever. Amen.

—KJV

[or]

Our Father in heaven,
hallowed be your name,
your kingdom come,
your will be done
 on earth as it is in heaven.
Give us today our daily bread.
Forgive us our debts,
 as we also have forgiven our debtors.
And lead us not into temptation,
but deliver us from the evil one.
For yours is the kingdom and the power
and the glory forever. Amen.

—NIV

Benediction

Go in peace,
and may the God of peace—
who through the blood of the eternal covenant
brought back from the dead our Lord Jesus,
that great Shepherd of the sheep,
equip you with everything good for doing his will,
and may he work in us what is pleasing to him,
through Jesus Christ, to whom be glory forever and ever.
AMEN.

—Hebrews 13:20-21

[or]

May the love of God and the peace of our Lord Jesus Christ
bless and console us,
and gently wipe every tear from our eyes:
in the name of the Father,
and of the Son, and of the Holy Spirit.
AMEN.

—OCF

[or]

May the peace of God,
which is beyond all understanding,
keep your hearts and minds
in the knowledge and love of God
and of his Son, our Lord Jesus Christ.
AMEN.

—*OCF*

[or]

May God in his infinite love and mercy
bring the whole church,
living and departed in the Lord Jesus,
to a joyful resurrection
and the fullfillment of God's eternal kingdom.
AMEN.

—*ASB*

Hymn and Recessional

[At a funeral, the casket should be removed to the back of the church (chapel). The minister and family members may precede or follow the casket. The congregation should sing a triumphant hymn during the recessional. At a memorial service, the congregation should sing a triumphant hymn after the benediction, closing the service.]

Funeral Service II

A Participatory Liturgy

Funeral services I and II are virtually identical in structure. The main difference between them is that II is a participatory service, providing more opportunity for the congregation to join vocally in the liturgy. In those congregations where the regular Sunday service is highly participatory, the funeral service should be likewise. Some people argue that since it is difficult for grieving people to express their faith without arousing deep emotion, a funeral liturgy should be spoken mainly by the officiant. However, a study of grief and the needs of grieving people points to the therapeutic value of vocal expression and the emotional release it affords.

When this participatory service is used, it obviously necessitates the use of a printed liturgy. There are many beautiful bulletin covers available for these printed liturgies. However, consideration should also be given to the use of the congregation's regular bulletin cover, if there is one. This may help the grieving people to recognize that this service is woven into the life of the believing community.

For extended commentary on the various parts of the funeral service, see pp. 73ff.

The Prelude

The Placing of the Pall (optional)

[When the pall is placed in the presence of the congregation, one of the following may be said in addition to or in place of the opening sentences.]

Leader: For all of you who were baptized into Christ
have clothed yourselves with Christ (Gal. 3:27).
In his/her baptism, _________ put on Christ;
in the day of Christ's coming,
he/she shall be clothed with Christ's glory.

[or]

Leader: All of us who were baptized into Christ Jesus
were baptized into his death.

We were therefore buried with him through baptism
into death
in order that, just as Christ was raised from the dead
through the glory of the Father, we too may live a new
life.
If we have been united with him like this in his death
we will certainly also be united with him in his
resurrection.

—*Romans 6:3-5*

People: Those who believe in him,
though they die, yet shall they live.

[A pall is placed over the coffin.]

Procession

Opening Sentences of Scripture

[One or several of the following sentences from Scripture may be used.]

Leader: The psalmist proclaims:

My heart is glad and my tongue rejoices;
my body also will rest secure,
because you will not abandon me to the grave,
nor will you let your Holy One see decay.

People: You have made known to me the path of life;
you will fill me with joy in your presence,
with eternal pleasures at your right hand.

—Psalm 16:9-11

Leader: God is our refuge and strength,
an ever-present help in trouble.

People: Therefore we will not fear.

—Psalm 46:1-2

Leader: Our help is in the name of the LORD,
the maker of heaven and earth.

People: Amen.

—Psalm 124:8

Leader: Jesus says:

I am the resurrection and the life.
He who believes in me will live, even though he dies;
and whoever lives and believes in me will never die.
Do you believe this?

People: Yes, Lord, we believe that you are the Christ,
the Son of God, who was to come into the world.

—John 11:25-26

Leader: The apostle Paul writes:

All of us who were baptized into Christ Jesus
were baptized into his death.

We were therefore buried with him through baptism into death
in order that, just as Christ was raised from the dead
through the glory of the Father,
we too may live a new life.

People: If we have been united with him like this in his death,
we will certainly also be united with him in his resurrection.

—Romans 6:3-5

Leader: If we live, we live to the Lord;
and if we die, we die to the Lord.

People: So, whether we live or die,
we belong to the Lord.

—Romans 14:8

Leader: We believe that Jesus died and rose again
and we believe that God will bring with Jesus
those who have fallen asleep in him.

People: And so we will be with the Lord forever.

—1 Thessalonians 4:14, 17, 18

Leader: What is your only comfort in life and in death?

People: That I am not my own, but belong,
body and soul, in life and in death,
to my faithful Savior Jesus Christ.

—Heidelberg Catechism, Q & A 1

Psalm, Hymn, or Spiritual Song

[congregation standing]

Call to Prayer

[Select one of the following to call the people to prayer.]

Brothers and sisters,
we have come together to renew our trust in Christ
who, by dying on the cross, has freed us from eternal death,
and, by rising, has opened for us the gates of heaven.
Let us pray *(or be thankful)* that our brother/sister
may share *(or shares)* in Christ's victory over death,
and let us pray for ourselves,
that the Lord may grant us
the gift of his loving consolation.

—*OCF*

[or]

Brothers and sisters,
Let us now turn our hearts to God in prayer
that he might strengthen our faith,
and grant us his peace and comfort.

[or]

We have gathered here in sorrow and in hope at the death of ________.
Let us now share our grief with God
and seek his comfort.

Opening Prayer(s)

[One or more of the following prayers may be offered, either in responsive form or by the officiant.]

Leader: Heavenly Father, our Creator and Redeemer,
in whose presence there is no darkness and no death:

People: We worship and adore you, the Living God.

Leader: Lord Jesus Christ, the resurrection and the life,
who tasted death for everyone
and who brought life and immortality to light:

People: We praise your name for victory over death and the grave.

Leader: Holy Spirit, author and giver of life,
comforter of all who sorrow:

People: We praise your name for the light and hope
of your presence within our hearts.

Leader: Before you, Holy and Triune God,
we offer our worship and adoration,
even in the face of death and the grave:

People: Blessing and honor
glory and power,
wisdom and strength,
belong to you, now and forever,
Amen.

—*TF*

Leader: O God, who brought us to birth,
you are always ready to hear us when we pray.
Even as sorrow pierces our hearts
at the death of __________, our brother/sister,
and we grope for words to express our pain;
you know all our needs before we ask,
and are ready to supply them all
out of the riches of your grace in Jesus Christ.
Show us now that grace,
that as we face the mystery of death
we may see the light and hope of eternity.
Speak to us once more that solemn message of life and death.

Help us to live as those prepared to die.
And when our days are ended,
enable us to die as those who go forth to live,
so that, living or dying,
our life may be in Jesus Christ, our risen Lord.

People: Amen.

—BS

Leader: Eternal God and Father,
gathered around your throne in glory
is that great company of all those who have kept the faith,
finished their race, and now rest from their labors.

People: We give you praise and thanks
that you have now received _______ into your presence.

Leader: Help us here on earth to believe that which we cannot see,
trusting in Christ who said,
"I go to prepare a place for you."

People: Bring us all at last with all your saints
into the joy of your eternal home,
through Jesus Christ our Lord.
Amen.

—BS

Leader: Eternal God, Shepherd of your people,
on this solemn occasion
we feel the fleeting passage of life;
and we know how fragile is our existence
on this tiny planet amid the spinning galaxies.
We confess with the prophet:

People: "All flesh is grass,
and all its glory is like the flowers of the field.
The grass withers and the flowers fall . . . ."

Leader: Yet we also confess:

People: "the word of our God stands forever."

Leader: Teach us to number our days,
that we may gain a heart of wisdom.
We look to you as frightened children look to their mother,
for you alone can comfort us.

People: Have mercy on us, O God.
See our tears and hear our cries,
and lead us all, as pilgrims,
through this valley of death's shadow
into the light of the resurrection of Jesus Christ
your Son, our Lord.
Amen.

Leader: God of grace and glory,
we remember before you this day
our brother/sister ________.
We thank you for giving him/her to us,
his/her family and friends,
to know and to love as a companion on this earthly pilgrimage.
In your boundless compassion, console us who mourn.
Give us faith to see in death the gateway of eternal life,
so that in quiet confidence
we may continue our course on earth,
until by your call,
we are united with those who have gone before;
through Jesus Christ our Lord.

People: Amen.

Leader: Most merciful God, whose wisdom is beyond our understanding:
deal graciously with ________ (names) in their grief.

Surround them with your love,
that they may not be overwhelmed by their loss,
but have confidence in your goodness,
and strength to meet the days to come;
through Jesus Christ our Lord.

People: Amen.

[At the death of a child]

Leader: Loving Father,
you are nearest to us when we need you most.
In this hour of sorrow we turn to you,
knowing that you love us
and trusting in your perfect wisdom.
We thank you for the gift of this child
and for his/her baptism into your church,
for the joy he/she gave all who knew him/her,
for the precious memories that will always abide with us,
and especially for the assurance that he/she lives forever
in the joy and peace of your presence;
through Jesus Christ our Lord.

People: Amen.

[Other prayers appropriate to specific circumstances can be found on pp. 194ff.]

Remembrance

[A family member(s) or friend(s) may offer a remembrance of the life and gifts of the deceased.]

Prayer for Illumination

[A prayer for illumination may be said by the officiant or in unison by the congregation before the Scriptures are read. Or the congregation may sing a prayer song, such as "O Word of God Incarnate" (Psalter Hymnal *279).]*

Eternal God,
your love for us is everlasting;
you alone can turn the shadow of death
into the brightness of morning light.
Help us to turn to you now with reverent and believing
hearts.
In the stillness of this solemn hour,
speak to us of eternal things,
so that, hearing the promises of Scripture,
we may have hope
and be lifted above the darkness and distress
into the light and peace of your presence,
through Jesus Christ our Lord.
Amen.
—*TF*

[or]

Lord Jesus Christ,
you are the living Word of God.
To whom else should we go?
For you have the words of eternal life.
As we listen to your word,
may your Spirit write its message on our hearts
and feed our souls with its nourishing truth.
Amen.

The Readings

[It is suggested that the Scriptures be read in this order: Old Testament, Psalm, New Testament, and Gospel. Usually no more than one passage should be read from each category. If one of the passages to be read will be the basis for the sermon, it should be read last, with an intervening psalm or hymn between it and the other passages read. The interval might also be an appropriate time for the Remembrance.]

Old Testament
Psalm *(read, recited, or sung)*
Epistle
Gospel
[Hymn, Psalm, or Remembrance]
Sermon Lesson

Sermon

[The brief sermon should proclaim the gospel and offer hope and comfort to the bereaved. Especially if there was no Remembrance, memories of the life of the deceased and expressions of gratitude to God for his/her life ought to be included.]

Psalm, Hymn, or Spiritual Song and/or Creed or other Statement of Faith

[A creed or other statement of faith is also suggested in the Committal service. If the Apostles' Creed is used for the funeral service, select a different statement of faith for the Committal (see pp. 187ff).]

All: I believe in God, the Father almighty,
creator of heaven and earth.

I believe in Jesus Christ, his only Son, our Lord,
who was conceived by the Holy Spirit
and born of the Virgin Mary.
He suffered under Pontius Pilate,
was crucified, died, and was buried;
he descended to hell.
On the third day he rose again from the dead.
He ascended to heaven,
and is seated at the right hand of God the Father almighty.
From there he will come again to judge the living and the dead.

I believe in the Holy Spirit,
the holy catholic church,
the communion of saints,
the forgiveness of sins,
the resurrection of the body,
and the life everlasting. Amen.

—*The Apostles' Creed*

Prayers

[One of the following prayers may be offered (see also pp. 94ff).]

Leader: Let us pray to our loving God
through Jesus Christ his Son, who said,
"I am the resurrection and the life."
Lord, you comforted Martha and Mary in their distress;
draw near to us who mourn for __________,
and dry the tears of those who weep.

People: Hear us, Lord.

Leader: You wept at the grave of Lazarus, your friend;
comfort us in our sorrow.

People: Hear us, Lord.

Leader: You raised the dead to life;
give eternal life to our brother/sister
through the power of your resurrection.

People: Hear us, Lord.

Leader: You promised paradise to the thief who repented;
we trust you to bring our brother/sister
into the joys of heaven.

People: Hear us, Lord.

Leader: Our brother/sister was washed in baptism
and nourished at your table;
may we see him/her through the eyes of faith
in the fellowship of your saints in glory.

People: Hear us, Lord.

Leader: Comfort us in our sorrows;
let our faith be our consolation
and eternal life our hope,
through Jesus Christ our Lord.

[A time of silent prayer may be offered.]

We pray this through Christ our Lord.

People: Amen.

—BCP

[or]

Leader: Almighty God,
you call your people together
into the household of faith.
Give to your whole church,
in heaven and on earth,
your light and your peace.
For this we pray to the Lord.

People: Hear our prayer, O Lord.

Leader: Grant that all who have been baptized
into Christ's death and resurrection
may die to sin and rise to newness of life,
and that through the gate of death and the grave
we may pass with him to our joyful resurrection.
For this we pray to the Lord.

People: Hear our prayer, O Lord.

Leader: Grant to us who are still in our pilgrimage,
and who walk as yet by faith,
that your Holy Spirit may lead us
in holiness and righteousness all our days.
For this we pray to the Lord.

People: Hear our prayer, O Lord.

Leader: Grant to us a spirit of true thanksgiving
for all the gifts and graces
which you gave to our brother/sister __________,
especially for __________
[here mention may be made of characteristics or service].
For all this we give you thanks, and pray to the Lord.

People: Hear our prayer, O Lord.

Leader: Grant to all who mourn
a sure confidence in your loving care,
that, casting all their sorrow on you,
they may know the consolation of your love.
For this we pray to the Lord.

People: Hear our prayer, O Lord.

Leader: Grant us grace
to entrust __________ to your never-failing love
which sustained him/her in this life.
Receive him/her into the arms of your mercy,
and remember him/her
according to the favor you bear toward your people.

People: Amen.

—*TF*

[or]

Leader: God of all grace,
you sent your Son, our Lord Jesus Christ,
to bring life and immortality into the world.
We give you thanks
that by his death he destroyed the grip of death
and by his resurrection he opened the kingdom of God
to all believers.
Make us confident that because he lives
we shall also live.

Deepen our conviction that neither death nor life,
nor things present nor things to come,
nor anything else in all creation
shall be able to separate us from your love.
Immerse us now in that love,
which is in Christ Jesus, our Lord
who lives with you and the Holy Spirit,
one God, now and forever.

People: Amen.

[The Prayer(s) may conclude with a Commendation.]

Commendation

Leader: Into your hands, O merciful Savior,
we commend your servant __________.
Acknowledge, we humbly pray,
a sheep of your own fold,
a lamb of your own flock,
a sinner of your own redeeming.
Receive him/her into the arms of your mercy,
into the blessed rest of everlasting peace,
and into the glorious company of the saints in light.

People: Amen.

—BCP

[or]

Leader: Holy God,
by your creative power
you gave us the gift of life,
and by your redeeming grace
you gave us new life in Jesus Christ.

We commend __________
to your merciful keeping
through faith in Jesus Christ our Lord
whose death saved us from sin
and whose resurrection brings us eternal life.

People: Amen.

—SMT

[or]

Leader: Into your hands, Father of all mercies,
we commend our brother/sister __________
in the sure and certain hope
that together with all who have died in Christ,
he/she will rise with him on the last day.
You opened the gates of eternal life to your servant;
now help us who remain to comfort one another
until we meet again
in the new heavens and the new earth.
Through Jesus Christ our Lord,

People: Amen.

—OCF

The Lord's Prayer

[When the Lord's Prayer is used at the end of the prayer(s), the prayer(s) will be closed with these words: "through Jesus Christ our Lord, who taught us to pray, saying . . . ."]

All: Our Father who art in heaven,
hallowed be thy name;
thy kingdom come;
thy will be done on earth as it is in heaven.
Give us this day our daily bread;
and forgive us our debts, as we forgive our debtors;
and lead us not into temptation, but deliver us from evil.

For thine is the kingdom, and the power,
and the glory, for ever. Amen.
—*KJV*

[or]

All: Our Father in heaven,
hallowed be your name,
your kingdom come,
your will be done
on earth as it is in heaven.
Give us today our daily bread.
Forgive us our debts,
as we also have forgiven our debtors.
And lead us not into temptation,
but deliver us from the evil one.
For yours is the kingdom and the power
and the glory forever. Amen.
—*NIV*

Benediction

Leader: Go in peace,
and may the God of peace,
who through the eternal covenant
brought back from the dead our Lord Jesus,
that great Shepherd of the sheep,
equip you with everything good for doing his will,
and may he work in us what is pleasing to him,
through Jesus Christ, to whom be glory forever and ever.

People: Amen.
—*Hebrews 13:20-21*

[or]

Leader: May the love of God and the peace of our Lord
Jesus Christ
bless and console us,
and gently wipe every tear from our eyes:
in the name of the Father,
and of the Son, and of the Holy Spirit.

People: Amen.

—*OCF*

[or]

Leader: May the peace of God
which is beyond all understanding,
keep your hearts and minds
in the knowledge of the love of God
and of his Son, our Lord Jesus Christ.

People: Amen.

—*OCF*

[or]

Leader: May God in his infinite love and mercy
bring the whole church,
living and departed in the Lord Jesus,
to a joyful resurrection
and the fulfillment of God's eternal kingdom.

People: Amen.

—*ASB*

Hymn and Recessional

[At a funeral, the casket should be removed from the church (chapel). The minister and family members may precede or follow the casket. The congregation should sing a triumphant hymn during the recessional. At a memorial service, the congregation should sing a triumphant hymn after the benediction closing the service.]

Funeral Service III

A Service of Scripture and Song

This service alternates Scripture and hymns that are chosen to move the congregation from contemplating the reality of death to rejoicing in the triumph over death; it ends with a vision of the saints in glory. This structure is suitable not only for a funeral service, but also (perhaps especially) for a memorial service.

Pacing is important. The liturgist and musicians should refrain from rushing the service by moving immediately from Scripture to song to Scripture. A few moments of quiet between reading and singing leaves time for the meaning to sink in for the worshiper.

The *opening hymn* sets much of the tone for the service. "For All the Saints" is especially useful because it expresses a sense of loss as well as a vision of the triumph of the redeemed. A number of other hymns suggested in the topical index of the *Psalter Hymnal* under "Funerals" are also appropriate. If a choir is available, an anthem may be substituted for or used in addition to the opening hymn.

The liturgist may either write an *opening prayer* or use one of the many prayers suggested in the two previous services or in the Additional Resources. In most cases, at this point in the service, people need time to move from the reality of death to the certainty of faith. Expressions of painful grief and humble gratitude for the life of the deceased are appropriate here, as well as calling upon the Lord to comfort those who have gathered.

The *readings and hymns* given are suggestions. When constructing a service, the liturgist and musicians should pay special attention to its *movement.* It is not enough merely to string together a number of Scripture readings and hymns, all of which have to do in some way with death and resurrection. One must pay attention to the movement of mood and the movement of faith from grief to triumph.

The *final reading and hymn* should lift the worshipers' eyes to glory. It is in this hope and with God's grace and peace that the worshipers can go to continue their mourning, resting in the assurance of Christ's victory over death.

Prelude

Procession

Opening Sentences of Scripture

[One or several of the following sentences from Scripture may be used.]

Leader: The psalmist proclaims:

My heart is glad, and my tongue rejoices;
my body also will rest secure,
because you will not abandon me to the grave,
nor will you let your Holy One see decay.

People: You have made known to me the path of life;
you will fill me with joy in your presence,
with eternal pleasures at your right hand.
—Psalm 16:9-11

Leader: God is our refuge and strength,
an ever-present help in trouble.

People: Therefore we will not fear.
—Psalm 46:1-2

Leader: Our help is in the name of the LORD,
the maker of heaven and earth.

People: Amen.
—Psalm 124:8

Leader: Jesus says:

I am the resurrection and the life.
He who believes in me will live, even though he dies;
and whoever lives and believes in me will never die.
Do you believe this?

People: Yes, Lord, we believe that you are the Christ,
the Son of God, who was to come into the world.
—John 11:25-26

Leader: The apostle Paul writes:

All of us who were baptized into Christ Jesus
were baptized into his death.
We were therefore buried with him through baptism into death
in order that, just as Christ was raised from the dead
through the glory of the Father,
we too may live a new life.

People: **If we have been united with him like this in his death
we will certainly also be united with him in his resurrection.**

—Romans 6:3-5

Leader: If we live, we live to the Lord;
and if we die, we die to the Lord.

People: **So, whether we live or die,
we belong to the Lord.**

—Romans 14:8

Leader: We believe that Jesus died and rose again,
and we believe that God will bring with Jesus
those who have fallen asleep in him.

People: **And so we will be with the Lord forever.**

—1 Thessalonians 4:14, 17, 18

Leader: What is your only comfort in life and in death?

People: **That I am not my own, but belong,
body and soul, in life and in death,
to my faithful Savior Jesus Christ.**

—Heidelberg Catechism Q & A 1

Hymn

"For All the Saints"

—Psalter Hymnal *505*

Prayer(s)

[One or more prayers may be offered.]

Leader: Eternal God, Shepherd of your people,
on this solemn occasion
we feel the fleeting passage of life;
and we know how fragile is our existence
on this tiny planet amid the spinning galaxies.
We confess with the prophet:

People: "All flesh is grass,
and all its glory is like the flowers of the field.
The grass withers and the flowers fall . . . ."

Leader: Yet we also confess:

People: "the word of our God stands forever."

Leader: Teach us to number our days,
that we may gain a heart of wisdom.
We look to you as frightened children look to their mother,
for you alone can comfort us.

People: Have mercy on us, O God.
See our tears and hear our cries,
and lead us all, as pilgrims,
through this valley of death's shadow
into the light of the resurrection of Jesus Christ,
your Son, our Lord.
Amen.

[Other prayers can be found in Funeral Services I or II or in the Additional Resources.]

First Reading

Psalm 90 or Isaiah 40:1-8

Hymn

"O God, Our Help in Ages Past"

—Psalter Hymnal *170 (alternate hymn:* PsH *491)*

Second Reading

John 5:19-30, John 11:17-44, or John 14:1-7

Hymn

"As Moses Raised the Serpent Up"

—Psalter Hymnal *219*

Third Reading

1 Corinthians 15:20-23, 35-36, 42-57, or 2 Corinthians 4:16-5:10

Hymn

"Praise the Savior Now and Ever"

—Psalter Hymnal *400 (alternate hymn:* PsH *387)*

Fourth Reading

[This reading should be selected by the officiant as the basis for the message to follow.]

Message

Prayer

[Prayers and commendations from Funeral Services I and II (pp. 94ff and 114ff) may be used.]

Psalm, Hymn, Spiritual Song and/or Creed or Confession of Faith

Reading Five

Revelation 7:9-17

Hymn

"By the Sea of Crystal"

—Psalter Hymnal *620*

Benediction

Leader: Go in peace,
and may the God of peace—
who through the eternal covenant
brought back from the dead our Lord Jesus,
that great Shepherd of the sheep,
equip you with everything good for doing his will,
and may he work in us what is pleasing to him,
through Jesus Christ, to whom be glory forever and ever.

People: Amen.

—Hebrews 13:20-21

[or]

Leader: May the love of God and the peace of our Lord Jesus Christ
bless and console us,
and gently wipe every tear from our eyes:
in the name of the Father,
and of the Son, and of the Holy Spirit.

People: Amen.

—OCF

[or]

Leader: May the peace of God,
which is beyond all understanding,
keep your hearts and minds
in the knowledge of the love of God
and of his Son, our Lord Jesus Christ.

People: Amen.

—OCF

[or]

Leader: May God in his infinite love and mercy
bring the whole church,
living and departed in the Lord Jesus,
to a joyful resurrection
and the fullfillment of God's eternal kingdom.

People: Amen.

—ASB

Committal Service

The committal is an extremely difficult, yet important part of the journey of grief that began with the death of the individual. The loved ones now come, at last, to that place where they will part with the earthly body of their beloved. We live in a death-denying culture that avoids the physical reality of death. Such denial is not healthy for grieving people. The earthly finality of the graveside is important to bring closure to that part of grief's journey that is ritualized in public. Therefore, the committal service is most appropriately held at the graveside. However, when circumstances such as weather or location make a graveside service difficult, the committal may take place at the end of the funeral service, before the benediction.

When should the committal take place? Pastors sometimes express legitimate concern over the fact that after lifting the grieving people's faith and hope to God in the funeral service, the wounds of grief are opened wide again at the inevitable pain of the graveside service. That is not, however, a decisive argument against a graveside committal after the funeral. The committal is just one of many times that grief's wounds will be reopened.

The family may also wish to consider holding the committal service before the funeral (which will then become, strictly speaking, a memorial service, since the body will not be present). This arrangement has several advantages. It eliminates the necessity of an often long or difficult journey by large numbers of people to the burial site, and it allows a smaller group of family and close friends to express their feelings in a less public setting.

In the *invitation* the officiant will give expression to the purpose for this committal rite, with sensitivity to the feelings of those present.

The *opening sentences of Scripture* will link the committal with the funeral or memorial service as celebrations of the hope we have through the death and resurrection of Jesus Christ.

The heart of the *committal* speaks of the earth and of the grave itself. Those in attendance need to face the reality of death. But worshipers also need to look beyond the earthly grave to the resurrection of the dead in the last day. It is this all-important link that makes even the committal an act of hope.

A number of formulas for the committal are offered here. The officiant can choose the one that seems most appropriate, or can link several of them together. The commendation can be used at this point, especially if it was not used at the end of the prayer at the funeral (see "Commendation" under Funeral Service I, p. 98).

A number of *prayers* are offered for use. The liturgist can either choose one or link several together appropriately. The last prayer is a very old and beautiful expression found in many funeral liturgies and is especially suitable to the somber mood of the committal service.

Again, the committal service is a very appropriate moment to express a common faith using the words of a *creed or other statement of faith.* Confessing their faith together lifts the mourners beyond the grave to the eternal promises of God. It is important that the officiant not assume that all those present will recall the words of even a familiar statement of faith—printed copies should be made available.

After the *benediction,* the doxology or another familiar hymn would be appropriate to give expression to our trust in God. Again, making printed copies available may be advisable.

Finally, before departing, a member of the family may wish to offer a few words—perhaps expressing gratitude to those gathered for their love and support and requesting their continued prayers. These words serve as a bridge between the committal service and as a time of fellowship among those who wish to linger for a brief time at the grave site.

The Invitation

[When the people have arrived at the place of committal, the minister shall say the following.]

The life which this child of God received is not destroyed by death. God has received him/her into eternal life.

[or]

Having respectfully followed the body of our brother/sister _________ to this, its final resting place here on earth, let us look to God who promises us eternal life.

[or]

Having worshiped God in faith and hope,
we now come to the moment of final parting.
There is sadness in parting,
but we take comfort in the hope
that one day we shall meet again
when the love of Christ, which conquers all things,
destroys even death itself.

The Opening Sentences of Scripture

[One or more of the following verses or another brief Scripture verse is read.]

We read in Scripture:

I know that my Redeemer lives,
and that in the end he will stand upon the earth.
—*Job 19:25*

Come, you who are blessed by my Father;
take your inheritance,
the kingdom prepared for you since the creation of the world.
—*Matthew 25:34*

This is the will of him who sent me,
that I shall lose none of all that he has given me,
but raise them up at the last day.

—John 6:39

Because I live, you also will live.

—John 14:19

If we live, we live to the Lord;
and if we die, we die to the Lord.
So, whether we live or die, we belong to the Lord.

—Romans 14:8

Our citizenship is in heaven.
And we eagerly await a Savior from there,
The Lord Jesus Christ.

—Philippians 3:20

Do not be afraid.
I am the First and the Last.
I am the Living One;
I was dead, and behold I am alive for ever and ever!

—Revelation 1:17-18

The Committal

[If the committal takes place at the burial site, the minister and others may cast soil on the casket after it has been lowered into the grave. If the casket is to be lowered after the people have left, the minister shall stand near or behind the casket gesturing toward it or placing a hand upon it. In either case, the minister says:]

As we mark the close of the earthly pilgrimage
of __________, our brother/sister,
we commit his/her body to the ground,
out of which we were formed,
and we commit his/her spirit to the care of God,
our Creator and Redeemer.

We commit his/her grieving family and friends
into God's loving arms
and into the care of the Christian community.
And we commit our life and future into God's care
in the sure and certain hope of the resurrection of the body
through Jesus Christ, our Lord.

[or]

In the sure and certain hope of the resurrection to eternal life, through our Lord Jesus Christ,
we commend to almighty God our brother/sister
__________,
and we commit his/her body *(or ashes)*
to the ground *(or resting place, or the deep)*:
earth to earth, ashes to ashes, dust to dust.
Blessed are the dead who die in the Lord, says the Spirit.
They rest from their labors, and their works follow them.

—BCP
—Revelation 14:13

[and/or]

Where, O death, is your victory?
Where, O death, is your sting?
Thanks be to God!
He gives us the victory through our Lord Jesus Christ.

—1 Corinthians 15:55, 57

[and/or, if the commendation was not included in the funeral service]

Into your hands, O merciful Savior,
we commend __________ *(or, the soul of __________)*.
Acknowledge, we humbly pray,
a sheep of your own fold,
a lamb of your own flock,
a sinner of your own redeeming.

Receive him/her into the arms of your mercy,
into the blessed rest of everlasting peace,
and into the glorious company of the saints in light.

—BCP

Since God has called our brother/sister __________
from this life to himself,
we commit his/her body *(or ashes)*
to the earth *(or the elements, the deep, its resting place)*
for we are dust and to dust we shall return.
But the Lord Jesus Christ will change our mortal bodies
to be like his in glory,
for he is risen, the firstborn of the dead.
So let us commend our brother/sister
(or, the soul of our brother/sister) to the Lord,
that the Lord may embrace him/her in love
and raise up his/her body on the last day.

—OCF

[For a child]

Heavenly Father, ever caring and gentle,
we commit to your loving arms this little one, __________,
who brought joy into our lives for so short a time.
Enfold him/her in life eternal.

—OCF

Prayer(s)

[One or more of the following prayers may be said.]

Almighty God,
Father of the whole family in heaven and on earth,
stand by those who sorrow;
that, as they lean on your strength,
they may be upheld,
and believe the good news of life beyond life;
through Jesus Christ our Lord.
AMEN.

—TF

God of boundless compassion,
our only sure comfort in distress,
look tenderly upon your children
overwhelmed by loss and sorrow.
Lighten our darkness with your presence
and assure us of your love.
Enable us to see beyond this grave and our grief
to your eternal kingdom,
promised to all who love you in Christ the Lord.
AMEN.

—TF

Gracious Father,
with heavy hearts
we bid final farewell to the earthly remains
of __________, our brother/sister.
Lift up our hearts to you by faith.
Help us to see death as a doorway to life,
and the grave, a resting place awaiting resurrection,
through Jesus Christ,
our risen Lord and coming King.
AMEN.

Grant, O Lord, to all who are bereaved *(or to __________)*
the spirit of faith and courage,
that they may have strength to meet the days to come
with courage and patience;
not sorrowing as those without hope,
but in thankful remembrance of your great goodness,
and in the joyful expectation of eternal life
with those they love,
through Jesus Christ our Lord.

—BCP

Lord God, whose days are without end
and whose mercies beyond counting,
keep us mindful
that life is short and the hour of death unknown.
May your Spirit guide our days on earth
in ways of holiness, peace, and justice,
that we may serve you
with all your people,
sure in faith, strong in hope, perfected in love.
And when our earthly journey is ended,
lead us rejoicing into your kingdom,
where you live for ever and ever.

—OCF

Merciful God, Father of our Lord Jesus Christ
who is the resurrection and the life:
Raise us, we humbly pray,
from the death of sin to the life of righteousness.
When we depart this life may we rest in your arms,
and at the resurrection receive that blessing
which your well-beloved Son shall pronounce:
"Come, you blessed of my Father,
receive the kingdom prepared for you
from the beginning of the world."
We ask this, merciful God,
through Jesus Christ our Mediator and Redeemer.
AMEN.

—BCP

O Lord, support us all the day
of this troubled life,
until the shadows lengthen,
and the evening comes,
and the busy world is hushed,
and the fever of life is over,
and our work is done.

Then in your mercy grant us
a safe lodging and a holy rest,
and peace at last;
through Jesus Christ our Lord.
AMEN.

[At the committal of a child]

Gracious God,
your Fatherly heart knows the ache we feel
as our little __________ is laid to rest.
Give us grace now to entrust him/her to your care,
great God and Father of us all,
and bring us all, when our earthly journey is ended,
to the joy and peace of your kingdom,
through Jesus Christ our Lord.
AMEN.

[or]

Loving God,
your beloved Son took children in his arms and blessed them.
Give us grace now, we pray,
that we may entrust __________
to your never-failing care and love,
and bring us all to your heavenly kingdom;
through Jesus Christ our Lord.
AMEN.

Statement of Faith

[If the Apostles' Creed has not been recited previously, it should be recited here. If the Creed was recited in the funeral, it would be appropriate here to make use of another statement of faith such as those suggested in Additional Resources, pages 187-193. It would also be appropriate to sing a familiar hymn.]

Benediction

[One or more of the following blessings may be said:]

The Lord bless you and keep you.
The Lord be kind and gracious to you.
The Lord look upon you with favor
and give you peace.
AMEN.

The LORD bless you and keep you;
the LORD make his face shine upon you
and be gracious to you;
the LORD turn his face toward you
and give you peace.
AMEN.

—*Numbers 6:24-26*

The peace of God,
which transcends all understanding,
guard your hearts and your minds
in Christ Jesus.

—*Philippians 4:7*

And may the blessing of almighty God,
Father, Son, and Holy Spirit,
remain with you always.
AMEN.

Hymn

[The committal service may conclude with the singing of the doxology or another hymn expressing peace and hope.]

ADDITIONAL RESOURCES

Scripture Readings

Psalms

The Psalms, the "prayer book of the church," are a rich source of expression for the feelings and the faith of God's people, and are therefore important to include in the ministry to those near death and in the funeral service. The Psalms, either sung or spoken, may be used in various parts of a funeral service and in other services of prayer. It is important that the Psalms used not only express faith and hope, but also give sensitive expression to the doubts and hurts of the people.

Psalm 16:1-2, 5-11

Keep me safe, O God,
  for in you I take refuge.
I said to the LORD, "You are my Lord;
  apart from you I have no good thing."

LORD, you have assigned me my portion and my cup;
  you have made my lot secure.
The boundary lines have fallen for me in pleasant places;
  surely I have a delightful inheritance.
I will praise the LORD, who counsels me;
  even at night my heart instructs me.
I have set the LORD always before me.
  Because he is at my right hand,
  I will not be shaken.

Therefore my heart is glad and my tongue rejoices;
  my body also will rest secure,
because you will not abandon me to the grave,
  nor will you let your Holy One see decay.

You have made known to me the path of life;
you will fill me with joy in your presence,
with eternal pleasures at your right hand.

Psalm 22:1-5, 19, 22-24

My God, my God, why have you forsaken me?
Why are you so far from saving me,
so far from the words of my groaning?
O my God, I cry out by day, but you do not answer,
by night, and am not silent.
Yet you are enthroned as the Holy One;
you are the praise of Israel.
In you our fathers put their trust;
they trusted and you delivered them.
They cried to you and were saved;
in you they trusted and were not disappointed.

But you, O LORD, be not far off;
O my Strength, come quickly to help me.

I will declare your name to my brothers;
in the congregation I will praise you.
You who fear the LORD, praise him!
All you descendants of Jacob, honor him!
Revere him, all you descendants of Israel!
For he has not despised or disdained
the suffering of the afflicted one;
he has not hidden his face from him
but has listened to his cry for help.

Psalm 23

The LORD is my shepherd, I shall not be in want.
He makes me lie down in green pastures,
he leads me beside quiet waters,
he restores my soul.
He guides me in paths of righteousness
for his name's sake.

Even though I walk
through the valley of the shadow of death,
I will fear no evil,
for you are with me,
your rod and your staff,
they comfort me.

You prepare a table before me
in the presence of my enemies.
You anoint my head with oil;
my cup overflows.
Surely goodness and love will follow me
all the days of my life,
and I will dwell in the house of the LORD
forever.

Psalm 25:1-7, 10, 14-18, 20-22

To you, O LORD, I lift up my soul;
in you I trust, O my God.
Do not let me be put to shame,
nor let my enemies triumph over me.
No one whose hope is in you
will ever be put to shame,
but they will be put to shame
who are treacherous without excuse.

Show me your ways, O LORD,
teach me your paths;
guide me in your truth and teach me,
for you are God my Savior,
and my hope is in you all day long.
Remember, O LORD, your great mercy and love,
for they are from of old.
Remember not the sins of my youth
and my rebellious ways;
according to your love remember me,
for you are good, O LORD.

All the ways of the LORD are loving and faithful
for those who keep the demands of his covenant.

The LORD confides in those who fear him;
he makes his covenant known to them.
My eyes are ever on the LORD,
for only he will release my feet from the snare.
Turn to me and be gracious to me,
for I am lonely and afflicted.
The troubles of my heart have multiplied;
free me from my anguish.
Look upon my affliction and my distress
and take away all my sins.

Guard my life and rescue me;
let me not be put to shame,
for I take refuge in you.
May integrity and uprightness protect me,
because my hope is in you.

Redeem Israel, O God,
from all their troubles!

Psalm 27:1-13

The LORD is my light and my salvation—
whom shall I fear?
The LORD is the stronghold of my life—
of whom shall I be afraid?
When evil men advance against me
to devour my flesh,
when my enemies and my foes attack me,
they will stumble and fall.
Though an army besiege me,
my heart will not fear;
though war break out against me,
even then will I be confident.

One thing I ask of the LORD,
 this is what I seek:
that I may dwell in the house of the LORD
 all the days of my life,
to gaze upon the beauty of the LORD
 and to seek him in his temple.
For in the day of trouble
 he will keep me safe in his dwelling;
he will hide me in the shelter of his tabernacle
 and set me high upon a rock.
Then my head will be exalted
 above the enemies who surround me;
at his tabernacle will I sacrifice with shouts of joy;
 I will sing and make music to the LORD.

Hear my voice when I call, O LORD;
 be merciful to me and answer me.
My heart says of you, "Seek his face!"
 Your face, LORD, I will seek.
Do not hide your face from me,
 do not turn your servant away in anger;
 you have been my helper.
Do not reject me or forsake me,
 O God my Savior.
Though my father and mother forsake me,
 the LORD will receive me.
Teach me your way, O LORD;
 lead me in a straight path
 because of my oppressors.
Do not turn me over to the desire of my foes,
 for false witnesses rise up against me,
 breathing out violence.

I am still confident of this:
 I will see the goodness of the LORD
 in the land of the living.

Psalm 46:1-5, 10-11

God is our refuge and strength,
 an ever-present help in trouble.
Therefore we will not fear, though the earth give way
 and the mountains fall into the heart of the sea,
though its waters roar and foam
 and the mountains quake with their surging.

There is a river whose streams make glad the city of God,
 the holy place where the Most High dwells.
God is within her, she will not fall;
 God will help her at break of day.

"Be still, and know that I am God;
 I will be exalted among the nations,
 I will be exalted in the earth."

The LORD Almighty is with us;
 the God of Jacob is our fortress.

Psalm 62

My soul finds rest in God alone;
 my salvation comes from him.
He alone is my rock and my salvation;
 he is my fortress, I will never be shaken.

How long will you assault a man?
 Would all of you throw him down—
 this leaning wall, this tottering fence?
They fully intend to topple him
 from his lofty place;
 they take delight in lies.
With their mouths they bless,
 but in their hearts they curse.

Find rest, O my soul, in God alone;
my hope comes from him.
He alone is my rock and my salvation;
he is my fortress, I will not be shaken.
My salvation and my honor depend on God;
he is my mighty rock, my refuge.
Trust in him at all times, O people;
pour out your hearts to him,
for God is our refuge.

Lowborn men are but a breath,
the highborn are but a lie;
if weighed on a balance, they are nothing;
together they are only a breath.
Do not trust in extortion
or take pride in stolen goods;
though your riches increase,
do not set your heart on them.

One thing God has spoken,
two things have I heard:
that you, O God, are strong,
and that you, O Lord, are loving.
Surely you will reward each person
according to what he has done.

Psalm 90

Lord, you have been our dwelling place
throughout all generations.
Before the mountains were born
or you brought forth the earth and the world,
from everlasting to everlasting you are God.

You turn men back to dust,
saying, "Return to dust, O sons of men."

For a thousand years in your sight
    are like a day that has just gone by,
    or like a watch in the night.
You sweep men away in the sleep of death;
    they are like the new grass of the morning—
though in the morning it springs up new,
    by evening it is dry and withered.

We are consumed by your anger
    and terrified by your indignation.
You have set our iniquities before you,
    our secret sins in the light of your presence.
All our days pass away under your wrath;
    we finish our years with a moan.
The length of our days is seventy years—
    or eighty, if we have the strength;
yet their span is but trouble and sorrow,
    for they quickly pass, and we fly away.

Who knows the power of your anger?
    For your wrath is as great as the fear that is due you.
Teach us to number our days aright,
    that we may gain a heart of wisdom.

Relent, O LORD! How long will it be?
    Have compassion on your servants.
Satisfy us in the morning with your unfailing love,
    that we may sing for joy and be glad all our days.
Make us glad for as many days as you have afflicted us,
    for as many years as we have seen trouble.
May your deeds be shown to your servants,
    your splendor to their children.

May the favor of the LORD our God rest upon us;
    establish the work of our hands for us—
    yes, establish the work of our hands.

Psalm 91

He who dwells in the shelter of the Most High
 will rest in the shadow of the Almighty.
I will say of the LORD, "He is my refuge and my fortress,
 my God, in whom I trust."

Surely he will save you from the fowler's snare
 and from the deadly pestilence.
He will cover you with his feathers,
 and under his wings you will find refuge;
 his faithfulness will be your shield and rampart.
You will not fear the terror of night,
 nor the arrow that flies by day,
nor the pestilence that stalks in the darkness,
 nor the plague that destroys at midday.

A thousand may fall at your side,
 ten thousand at your right hand,
 but it will not come near you.
You will only observe with your eyes
 and see the punishment of the wicked.

If you make the Most High your dwelling—
 even the LORD, who is my refuge—
then no harm will befall you,
 no disaster will come near your tent.
For he will command his angels concerning you
 to guard you in all your ways;
they will lift you up in their hands,
 so that you will not strike your foot against a stone.
You will tread upon the lion and the cobra;
 you will trample the great lion and the serpent.

"Because he loves me," says the LORD, "I will rescue him;
 I will protect him, for he acknowledges my name.
He will call upon me, and I will answer him;
 I will be with him in trouble,
 I will deliver him and honor him.

With long life will I satisfy him
 and show him my salvation."

Psalm 103

Praise the LORD, O my soul;
 all my inmost being, praise his holy name.
Praise the LORD, O my soul,
 and forget not all his benefits—
who forgives all your sins
 and heals all your diseases,
who redeems your life from the pit
 and crowns you with love and compassion,
who satisfies your desires with good things
 so that your youth is renewed like the eagle's.

The LORD works righteousness
 and justice for all the oppressed.

He made known his ways to Moses,
 his deeds to the people of Israel:
The LORD is compassionate and gracious,
 slow to anger, abounding in love.
He will not always accuse,
 nor will he harbor his anger forever;
he does not treat us as our sins deserve
 or repay us according to our iniquities.
For as high as the heavens are above the earth,
 so great is his love for those who fear him;
as far as the east is from the west,
 so far has he removed our transgressions from us.
As a father has compassion on his children,
 so the LORD has compassion on those who fear him;
for he knows how we are formed,
 he remembers that we are dust.

As for man, his days are like grass,
he flourishes like a flower of the field;
the wind blows over it and it is gone,
and its place remembers it no more.
But from everlasting to everlasting
the LORD's love is with those who fear him,
and his righteousness with their children's children—
with those who keep his covenant
and remember to obey his precepts.

The LORD has established his throne in heaven,
and his kingdom rules over all.

Praise the LORD, you his angels,
you mighty ones who do his bidding,
who obey his word.

Praise the LORD, all his heavenly hosts,
you his servants who do his will.
Praise the LORD, all his works
everywhere in his dominion.

Praise the LORD, O my soul.

Psalm 116

I love the LORD, for he heard my voice;
he heard my cry for mercy.
Because he turned his ear to me,
I will call on him as long as I live.

The cords of death entangled me,
the anguish of the grave came upon me;
I was overcome by trouble and sorrow.
Then I called on the name of the LORD:
"O LORD, save me!"

The LORD is gracious and righteous;
    our God is full of compassion.
The LORD protects the simplehearted;
    when I was in great need, he saved me.

Be at rest once more, O my soul,
    for the LORD has been good to you.

For you, O LORD, have delivered my soul from death,
    my eyes from tears,
    my feet from stumbling,
that I may walk before the LORD
    in the land of the living.
I believed; therefore I said,
    "I am greatly afflicted."
And in my dismay I said,
    "All men are liars."
How can I repay the LORD
    for all his goodness to me?
I will lift up the cup of salvation
    and call on the name of the LORD.
I will fulfill my vows to the LORD
    in the presence of all his people.

Precious in the sight of the LORD
    is the death of his saints.
O LORD, truly I am your servant;
    I am your servant, the son of your maidservant;
    you have freed me from my chains.

I will sacrifice a thank offering to you
    and call on the name of the LORD.
I will fulfill my vows to the LORD
    in the presence of all his people,
in the courts of the house of the LORD—
    in your midst, O Jerusalem.

Praise the LORD.

Psalm 121

I lift up my eyes to the hills—
  where does my help come from?
My help comes from the LORD,
  the Maker of heaven and earth.

He will not let your foot slip—
  he who watches over you will not slumber;
indeed, he who watches over Israel
  will neither slumber nor sleep.

The LORD watches over you—
  the LORD is your shade at your right hand;
the sun will not harm you by day,
  nor the moon by night.

The LORD will keep you from all harm—
  he will watch over your life;
the LORD will watch over your coming and going
  both now and forevermore.

Psalm 130

Out of the depths I cry to you, O LORD;
  O Lord, hear my voice.
Let your ears be attentive
  to my cry for mercy.

If you, O LORD, kept a record of sins,
  O Lord, who could stand?
But with you there is forgiveness;
  therefore you are feared.

I wait for the LORD, my soul waits,
and in his word I put my hope.

My soul waits for the Lord
  more than watchmen wait for the morning,
  more than watchmen wait for the morning.

O Israel, put your hope in the LORD,
for with the LORD is unfailing love
and with him is full redemption.
He himself will redeem Israel
from all their sins.

Psalm 131

My heart is not proud, O LORD,
my eyes are not haughty;
I do not concern myself with great matters
or things too wonderful for me.
But I have stilled and quieted my soul;
like a weaned child with its mother,
like a weaned child is my soul within me.

O Israel, put your hope in the LORD
both now and forevermore.

Psalm 139

O LORD, you have searched me
and you know me.
You know when I sit and when I rise;
you perceive my thoughts from afar.
You discern my going out and my lying down;
you are familiar with all my ways.
Before a word is on my tongue
you know it completely, O LORD.

You hem me in—behind and before;
you have laid your hand upon me.
Such knowledge is too wonderful for me,
too lofty for me to attain.

Where can I go from your Spirit?
Where can I flee from your presence?

If I go up to the heavens, you are there;
if I make my bed in the depths, you are there.

If I rise on the wings of the dawn,
    if I settle on the far side of the sea,
even there your hand will guide me,
    your right hand will hold me fast.

If I say, "Surely the darkness will hide me
    and the light become night around me,"
even the darkness will not be dark to you;
    the night will shine like the day,
    for darkness is as light to you.

For you created my inmost being;
    you knit me together in my mother's womb.
I praise you because I am fearfully and wonderfully made;
    your works are wonderful,
    I know that full well.
My frame was not hidden from you
    when I was made in the secret place.
When I was woven together in the depths of the earth,
    your eyes saw my unformed body.
All the days ordained for me
    were written in your book
    before one of them came to be.

How precious to me are your thoughts, O God!
    How vast is the sum of them!
Were I to count them,
    they would outnumber the grains of sand.
When I awake,
    I am still with you.

If only you would slay the wicked, O God!
    Away from me, you bloodthirsty men!
They speak of you with evil intent;
    your adversaries misuse your name.
Do I not hate those who hate you, O LORD,
    and abhor those who rise up against you?

I have nothing but hatred for them;
I count them my enemies.

Search me, O God, and know my heart;
test me and know my anxious thoughts.
See if there is any offensive way in me,
and lead me in the way everlasting.

Psalm 146

Praise the LORD.

Praise the LORD, O my soul.
I will praise the LORD all my life;
I will sing praise to my God as long as I live.

Do not put your trust in princes,
in mortal men, who cannot save.
When their spirit departs, they return to the ground;
on that very day their plans come to nothing.

Blessed is he whose help is the God of Jacob,
whose hope is in the LORD his God,
the Maker of heaven and earth,
the sea, and everything in them—
the LORD, who remains faithful forever.
He upholds the cause of the oppressed
and gives food to the hungry.
The LORD sets prisoners free,
the LORD gives sight to the blind,
the LORD lifts up those who are bowed down,
the LORD loves the righteous.
The LORD watches over the alien
and sustains the fatherless and the widow,
but he frustrates the ways of the wicked.

The LORD reigns forever,
your God, O Zion, for all generations.

Praise the LORD.

Other Old Testament Passages

2 Samuel 12:18-24

On the seventh day the child died. David's servants were afraid to tell him that the child was dead, for they thought, "While the child was still living, we spoke to David but he would not listen to us. How can we tell him the child is dead? He may do something desperate."

David noticed that his servants were whispering among themselves and he realized the child was dead. "Is the child dead?" he asked.

"Yes," they replied, "he is dead."

Then David got up from the ground. After he had washed, put on lotions and changed his clothes, he went into the house of the LORD and worshiped. Then he went to his own house, and at his request they served him food, and he ate.

His servants asked him, "Why are you acting this way? While the child was alive, you fasted and wept, but now that the child is dead, you get up and eat!"

He answered, "While the child was still alive, I fasted and wept. I thought, 'Who knows? The LORD may be gracious to me and let the child live.' But now that he is dead, why should I fast? Can I bring him back again? I will go to him, but he will not return to me."

Then David comforted his wife Bathsheba, and he went to her and lay with her. She gave birth to a son, and they named him Solomon. The LORD loved him.

Job 19:25-27

I know that my Redeemer lives,
    and that in the end he will stand upon the earth.
And after my skin has been destroyed,
    yet in my flesh I will see God;

I myself will see him
with my own eyes—I, and not another.
How my heart yearns within me!

Ecclesiastes 3:1-15 [appropriate for those whose faith is unknown]

There is a time for everything,
and a season for every activity under heaven:

a time to be born and a time to die,
a time to plant and a time to uproot,
a time to kill and a time to heal,
a time to tear down and a time to build,
a time to weep and a time to laugh,
a time to mourn and a time to dance,
a time to scatter stones and a time to gather them,
a time to embrace and a time to refrain,
a time to search and a time to give up,
a time to keep and a time to throw away,
a time to tear and a time to mend,
a time to be silent and a time to speak,
a time to love and a time to hate,
a time for war and a time for peace.

What does the worker gain from his toil? I have seen the burden God has laid on men. He has made everything beautiful in its time. He has also set eternity in the hearts of men; yet they cannot fathom what God has done from beginning to end. I know that there is nothing better for men than to be happy and do good while they live. That everyone may eat and drink, and find satisfaction in all his toil—this is the gift of God. I know that everything God does will endure forever; nothing can be added to it and nothing taken from it. God does it so that men will revere him.

Whatever is has already been,
and what will be has been before;
and God will call the past to account.

Isaiah 25:6, 7-9

On this mountain the LORD Almighty will prepare
 a feast of rich food for all peoples.
On this mountain he will destroy
 the shroud that enfolds all peoples,
the sheet that covers all nations;
 he will swallow up death forever.
The Sovereign LORD will wipe away the tears
 from all faces;
he will remove the disgrace of his people
 from all the earth.
 The LORD has spoken.

In that day they will say,

"Surely this is our God;
 we trusted in him, and he saved us.
This is the LORD, we trusted in him;
 let us rejoice and be glad in his salvation."

Isaiah 26:1-4, 12, 16-17, 19

In that day this song will be sung in the land of Judah:

We have a strong city;
 God makes salvation
 its walls and ramparts.
Open the gates
 that the righteous nation may enter,
 the nation that keeps faith.
You will keep in perfect peace
 him whose mind is steadfast,
 because he trusts in you.
Trust in the LORD forever,
 for the LORD, the LORD, is the Rock eternal.

LORD, you establish peace for us;
 all that we have accomplished you have done for us.

LORD, they came to you in their distress;
when you disciplined them,
they could barely whisper a prayer.
As a woman with child and about to give birth
writhes and cries out in her pain,
so were we in your presence, O LORD.

But your dead will live;
their bodies will rise.
You who dwell in the dust,
wake up and shout for joy.
Your dew is like the dew of the morning;
the earth will give birth to her dead.

Isaiah 35

The desert and the parched land will be glad;
the wilderness will rejoice and blossom.
Like the crocus, it will burst into bloom;
it will rejoice greatly and shout for joy.
The glory of Lebanon will be given to it,
the splendor of Carmel and Sharon;
they will see the glory of the LORD,
the splendor of our God.

Strengthen the feeble hands,
steady the knees that give way;
say to those with fearful hearts,
"Be strong, do not fear;
your God will come,
he will come with vengeance;
with divine retribution
he will come to save you."

Then will the eyes of the blind be opened
and the ears of the deaf unstopped.
Then will the lame leap like a deer,
and the mute tongue shout for joy.

Water will gush forth in the wilderness
and streams in the desert.
The burning sand will become a pool,
the thirsty ground bubbling springs.
In the haunts where jackals once lay,
grass and reeds and papyrus will grow.

And a highway will be there;
it will be called the Way of Holiness.
The unclean will not journey on it;
it will be for those who walk in that Way;
wicked fools will not go about on it.
No lion will be there,
nor will any ferocious beast get up on it;
they will not be found there.
But only the redeemed will walk there,
and the ransomed of the LORD will return.
They will enter Zion with singing;
everlasting joy will crown their heads.
Gladness and joy will overtake them,
and sorrow and sighing will flee away.

Isaiah 40:1-11

Comfort, comfort my people,
says your God.
Speak tenderly to Jerusalem,
and proclaim to her
that her hard service has been completed,
that her sin has been paid for,
that she has received from the LORD's hand
double for all her sins.

A voice of one calling:
"In the desert prepare
the way for the LORD;
make straight in the wilderness
a highway for our God.

Every valley shall be raised up,
  every mountain and hill made low;
the rough ground shall become level,
  the rugged places a plain.
And the glory of the LORD will be revealed,
  and all mankind together will see it.
    For the mouth of the LORD has spoken."

A voice says, "Cry out."
  And I said, "What shall I cry?"

"All men are like grass,
  and all their glory is like the flowers of the field.
The grass withers and the flowers fall,
  because the breath of the LORD blows on them.
  Surely the people are grass.
The grass withers and the flowers fall,
  but the word of our God stands forever."

You who bring good tidings to Zion,
  go up on a high mountain.
You who bring good tidings to Jerusalem,
  lift up your voice with a shout,
lift it up, do not be afraid;
  say to the towns of Judah,
  "Here is your God!"
See, the Sovereign LORD comes with power,
  and his arm rules for him.
See, his reward is with him,
  and his recompense accompanies him.

He tends his flock like a shepherd:
  He gathers the lambs in his arms
and carries them close to his heart;
  he gently leads those that have young.

Isaiah 40:28-31

Do you not know?
  Have you not heard?
The LORD is the everlasting God,
  the Creator of the ends of the earth.
He will not grow tired or weary,
  and his understanding no one can fathom.
He gives strength to the weary
  and increases the power of the weak.
Even youths grow tired and weary,
  and young men stumble and fall;
but those who hope in the LORD
  will renew their strength.
They will soar on wings like eagles;
  they will run and not grow weary,
  they will walk and not be faint.

Isaiah 43:1-3, 5-7

But now, this is what the LORD says—
  he who created you, O Jacob,
  he who formed you, O Israel:
"Fear not, for I have redeemed you;
  I have summoned you by name; you are mine.
When you pass through the waters,
  I will be with you;
and when you pass through the rivers,
  they will not sweep over you.
When you walk through the fire,
  you will not be burned;
  the flames will not set you ablaze.
For I am the LORD, your God,
  the Holy One of Israel, your Savior.

Do not be afraid, for I am with you;
  I will bring your children from the east
  and gather you from the west.

I will say to the north, 'Give them up!'
    and to the south, 'Do not hold them back.'
Bring my sons from afar
    and my daughters from the ends of the earth—
everyone who is called by my name,
    whom I created for my glory,
    whom I formed and made."

Isaiah 65:17-25 [appropriate at the death of a child]

"Behold, I will create
    new heavens and a new earth.
The former things will not be remembered,
    nor will they come to mind.
But be glad and rejoice forever
    in what I will create,
for I will create Jerusalem to be a delight
    and its people a joy.
I will rejoice over Jerusalem
    and take delight in my people;
the sound of weeping and of crying
    will be heard in it no more.

"Never again will there be in it
    an infant who lives but a few days,
    or an old man who does not live out his years;
he who dies at a hundred
    will be thought a mere youth;
he who fails to reach a hundred
    will be considered accursed.
They will build houses and dwell in them;
    they will plant vineyards and eat their fruit.
No longer will they build houses and others live in them,
    or plant and others eat.

For as the days of a tree,
so will be the days of my people;
my chosen ones will long enjoy
the works of their hands.
They will not toil in vain
or bear children doomed to misfortune;
for they will be a people blessed by the LORD,
they and their descendants with them.
Before they call I will answer;
while they are still speaking I will hear.
The wolf and the lamb will feed together,
and the lion will eat straw like the ox,
but dust will be the serpent's food.
They will neither harm nor destroy
on all my holy mountain,"
says the LORD.

Lamentations 3:1-9, 17-26

I am the man who has seen affliction
by the rod of his wrath.
He has driven me away and made me walk
in darkness rather than light;
indeed, he has turned his hand against me
again and again, all day long.
He has made my skin and my flesh grow old
and has broken my bones.
He has besieged me and surrounded me
with bitterness and hardship.
He has made me dwell in darkness
like those long dead.

He has walled me in so I cannot escape;
he has weighed me down with chains.
Even when I call out or cry for help,
he shuts out my prayer.

He has barred my way with blocks of stone;
he has made my paths crooked.

I have been deprived of peace;
I have forgotten what prosperity is.
So I say, "My splendor is gone
and all that I had hoped from the LORD."

I remember my affliction and my wandering,
the bitterness and the gall.
I well remember them,
and my soul is downcast within me.
Yet this I call to mind
and therefore I have hope:

Because of the LORD's great love we are not consumed,
for his compassions never fail.
They are new every morning;
great is your faithfulness.
I say to myself, "The LORD is my portion;
therefore I will wait for him."

The LORD is good to those whose hope is in him,
to the one who seeks him;
it is good to wait quietly
for the salvation of the LORD.

Zechariah 8:1-8 [appropriate at the death of a child]

Again the word of the LORD Almighty came to me. This is what the LORD Almighty says: "I am very jealous for Zion; I am burning with jealousy for her."

This is what the LORD says: "I will return to Zion and dwell in Jerusalem. Then Jerusalem will be called the City of Truth, and the mountain of the LORD Almighty will be called the Holy Mountain."

This is what the LORD Almighty says: "Once again men and women of ripe old age will sit in the streets of Jerusalem, each with cane in hand because of his age. The city streets will be filled with boys and girls playing there."

This is what the LORD Almighty says: "It may seem marvelous to the remnant of this people at that time, but will it seem marvelous to me?" declares the LORD Almighty.

This is what the LORD Almighty says: "I will save my people from the countries of the east and the west. I will bring them back to live in Jerusalem; they will be my people, and I will be faithful and righteous to them as their God."

New Testament Gospels

[Optional verses will be bracketed.]

Matthew 5:1-12

Now when he saw the crowds, he went up on a mountainside and sat down. His disciples came to him, and he began to teach them, saying:

"Blessed are the poor in spirit,
  for theirs is the kingdom of heaven.
Blessed are those who mourn,
  for they will be comforted.
Blessed are the meek,
  for they will inherit the earth.
Blessed are those who hunger and thirst for righteousness,
  for they will be filled.
Blessed are the merciful,
  for they will be shown mercy.
Blessed are the pure in heart,
  for they will see God.
Blessed are the peacemakers,
  for they will be called sons of God.
Blessed are those who are persecuted because of righteousness,
  for theirs is the kingdom of heaven.

"Blessed are you when people insult you, persecute you and falsely say all kinds of evil against you because of me. Rejoice and be glad, because great is your reward in heaven."

Matthew 11:25-30

At that time Jesus said, "I praise you, Father, Lord of heaven and earth, because you have hidden these things from the wise and learned, and revealed them to little children. Yes, Father, for this was your good pleasure.

"All things have been committed to me by my Father. No one knows the Son except the Father, and no one knows the Father except the Son and those to whom the Son chooses to reveal him.

"Come to me, all you who are weary and burdened, and I will give you rest. Take my yoke upon you and learn from me, for I am gentle and humble in heart, and you will find rest for your souls. For my yoke is easy and my burden is light."

Matthew 18:1-5, 10 [appropriate at the death of a child]

At that time the disciples came to Jesus and asked, "Who is the greatest in the kingdom of heaven?"

He called a little child and had him stand among them. And he said: "I tell you the truth, unless you change and become like little children, you will never enter the kingdom of heaven. Therefore, whoever humbles himself like this child is the greatest in the kingdom of heaven. And whoever welcomes a little child like this in my name welcomes me.

"See that you do not look down on one of these little ones. For I tell you that their angels in heaven always see the face of my Father in heaven."

Matthew 25:31-46 [appropriate for those whose faith is unknown]

"When the Son of Man comes in his glory, and all the angels with him, he will sit on his throne in heavenly glory. All the nations will be gathered before him, and he will separate the people one from another as a shepherd separates the sheep from the goats. He will put the sheep on his right and the goats on his left.

"Then the King will say to those on his right, 'Come, you who are blessed by my Father; take your inheritance, the kingdom prepared for you since the creation of the world. For I was hungry and you gave me something to eat, I was thirsty and you gave me something to drink, I was a stranger and you invited me in, I needed clothes and you clothed me, I was sick and you looked after me, I was in prison and you came to visit me.'

"Then the righteous will answer him, 'Lord, when did we see you hungry and feed you, or thirsty and give you something to drink? When did we see you a stranger and invite you in, or needing clothes and clothe you? When did we see you sick or in prison and go to visit you?'

"The King will reply, 'I tell you the truth, whatever you did for one of the least of these brothers of mine, you did for me.'

"Then he will say to those on his left, 'Depart from me, you who are cursed, into the eternal fire prepared for the devil and his angels. For I was hungry and you gave me nothing to eat, I was thirsty and you gave me nothing to drink, I was a stranger and you did not invite me in, I needed clothes and you did not clothe me, I was sick and in prison and you did not look after me.'

"They also will answer, 'Lord, when did we see you hungry or thirsty or a stranger or needing clothes or sick or in prison, and did not help you?'

"He will reply, 'I tell you the truth, whatever you did not do for one of the least of these, you did not do for me.'

"Then they will go away to eternal punishment, but the righteous to eternal life."

Mark 10:13-16 [appropriate at the death of a child]

People were bringing little children to Jesus to have him touch them, but the disciples rebuked them. When Jesus saw this, he was indignant. He said to them, "Let the little children come to me, and do not hinder them, for the kingdom of God belongs to such as these. I tell you the truth, anyone who will not receive the kingdom of God like a little child will never enter it." And he took the children in his arms, put his hands on them and blessed them.

Luke 7:11-17

Soon afterward, Jesus went to a town called Nain, and his disciples and a large crowd went along with him. As he approached the town gate, a dead person was being carried out—the only son of his mother, and she was a widow. And a large crowd from the town was with her. When the Lord saw her, his heart went out to her and he said, "Don't cry."

Then he went up and touched the coffin, and those carrying it stood still. He said, "Young man, I say to you, get up!" The dead man sat up and began to talk, and Jesus gave him back to his mother.

They were all filled with awe and praised God. "A great prophet has appeared among us," they said. "God has come to help his people." This news about Jesus spread throughout Judea and the surrounding country.

Luke 23:33, 39-43

When they came to the place called the Skull, there they crucified him, along with the criminals—one on his right, the other on his left.

One of the criminals who hung there hurled insults at him: "Aren't you the Christ? Save yourself and us!"

But the other criminal rebuked him. "Don't you fear God," he said, "since you are under the same sentence? We are punished justly, for we are getting what our deeds deserve. But this man has done nothing wrong."

Then he said, "Jesus, remember me when you come into your kingdom."

Jesus answered him, "I tell you the truth, today you will be with me in paradise."

Luke 23:44-46, 52-53 (or use 23:44-46, 50, 52-53)

It was now about the sixth hour, and darkness came over the whole land until the ninth hour, for the sun stopped shining. And the curtain of the temple was torn in two. Jesus called out with a loud voice, "Father, into your hands I commit my spirit." When he had said this, he breathed his last.

[Now there was a man named Joseph, a member of the Council, a good and upright man.] Going to Pilate, he asked for Jesus' body. Then he took it down, wrapped it in linen cloth and placed it in a tomb cut in the rock, one in which no one had yet been laid.

Luke 24:1-6

On the first day of the week, very early in the morning, the women took the spices they had prepared and went to the tomb. They found the stone rolled away from the tomb, but when they entered, they did not find the body of the Lord

Jesus. While they were wondering about this, suddenly two men in clothes that gleamed like lightning stood beside them. In their fright the women bowed down with their faces to the ground, but the men said to them, "Why do you look for the living among the dead? He is not here; he has risen!"

John 5:24-29

"I tell you the truth, whoever hears my word and believes him who sent me has eternal life and will not be condemned; he has crossed over from death to life. I tell you the truth, a time is coming and has now come when the dead will hear the voice of the Son of God and those who hear will live. For as the Father has life in himself, so he has granted the Son to have life in himself. And he has given him authority to judge because he is the Son of Man.

"Do not be amazed at this, for a time is coming when all who are in their graves will hear his voice and come out—those who have done good will rise to live, and those who have done evil will rise to be condemned."

John 6:37-40

"All that the Father gives me will come to me, and whoever comes to me I will never drive away. For I have come down from heaven not to do my will but to do the will of him who sent me. And this is the will of him who sent me, that I shall lose none of all that he has given me, but raise them up at the last day. For my Father's will is that everyone who looks to the Son and believes in him shall have eternal life, and I will raise him up at the last day."

John 11:17-27 (or use verses 21-27 only)

[On his arrival, Jesus found that Lazarus had already been in the tomb for four days. Bethany was less than two miles from Jerusalem, and many Jews had come to Martha and

Mary to comfort them in the loss of their brother. When Martha heard that Jesus was coming, she went out to meet him, but Mary stayed at home.]

"Lord," Martha said to Jesus, "if you had been here, my brother would not have died. But I know that even now God will give you whatever you ask."

Jesus said to her, "Your brother will rise again."

Martha answered, "I know he will rise again in the resurrection at the last day."

Jesus said to her, "I am the resurrection and the life. He who believes in me will live, even though he dies; and whoever lives and believes in me will never die. Do you believe this?"

"Yes, Lord," she told him, "I believe that you are the Christ, the Son of God, who was to come into the world."

John 11:32-45

When Mary reached the place where Jesus was and saw him, she fell at his feet and said, "Lord, if you had been here, my brother would not have died."

When Jesus saw her weeping, and the Jews who had come along with her also weeping, he was deeply moved in spirit and troubled. "Where have you laid him?" he asked.

"Come and see, Lord," they replied.

Jesus wept.

Then the Jews said, "See how he loved him!"

But some of them said, "Could not he who opened the eyes of the blind man have kept this man from dying?"

Jesus, once more deeply moved, came to the tomb. It was a cave with a stone laid across the entrance. "Take away the stone," he said.

"But, Lord," said Martha, the sister of the dead man, "by this time there is a bad odor, for he has been there four days."

Then Jesus said, "Did I not tell you that if you believed, you would see the glory of God?"

So they took away the stone. Then Jesus looked up and said, "Father, I thank you that you have heard me. I knew that you always hear me, but I said this for the benefit of the people standing here, that they may believe that you sent me."

When he had said this, Jesus called in a loud voice, "Lazarus, come out!" The dead man came out, his hands and feet wrapped with strips of linen, and a cloth around his face.

Jesus said to them, "Take off the grave clothes and let him go."

Therefore many of the Jews who had come to visit Mary, and had seen what Jesus did, put their faith in him.

John 12:23-26

Jesus replied, "The hour has come for the Son of Man to be glorified. I tell you the truth, unless a kernel of wheat falls to the ground and dies, it remains only a single seed. But if it dies, it produces many seeds. The man who loves his life will lose it, while the man who hates his life in this world will keep it for eternal life. Whoever serves me must follow me; and where I am, my servant also will be. My Father will honor the one who serves me.

John 14:1-6

"Do not let your hearts be troubled. Trust in God; trust also in me. In my Father's house are many rooms; if it were not so, I would have told you. I am going there to prepare a place for you. And if I go and prepare a place for you, I will come back and take you to be with me that you also may be where I am. You know the way to the place where I am going."

Thomas said to him, "Lord, we don't know where you are going, so how can we know the way?"

Jesus answered, "I am the way and the truth and the life. No one comes to the Father except through me.

New Testament Epistles

[Optional verses will be bracketed.]

Acts 10:34-43 (or use 34-36, 42-43)

Then Peter began to speak: "I now realize how true it is that God does not show favoritism but accepts men from every nation who fear him and do what is right. You know the message God sent to the people of Israel, telling the good news of peace through Jesus Christ, who is Lord of all. [You know what has happened throughout Judea, beginning in Galilee after the baptism that John preached—how God anointed Jesus of Nazareth with the Holy Spirit and power, and how he went around doing good and healing all who were under the power of the devil, because God was with him.

"We are witnesses of everything he did in the country of the Jews and in Jerusalem. They killed him by hanging him on a tree, but God raised him from the dead on the third day and caused him to be seen. He was not seen by all the people, but by witnesses whom God had already chosen—by us who ate and drank with him after he rose from the dead.] He commanded us to preach to the people and to testify that he is the one whom God appointed as judge of the living and the dead. All the prophets testify about him that everyone who believes in him receives forgiveness of sins through his name."

Romans 2:12-16 [appropriate for those whose faith is unknown]

All who sin apart from the law will also perish apart from the law, and all who sin under the law will be judged by the law. For it is not those who hear the law who are righteous in God's sight, but it is those who obey the law who will be declared righteous. (Indeed, when Gentiles, who do not have the law, do by nature things required by the law, they are a law for themselves, even though they do not have the law, since they show that the requirements of the law are written on their hearts, their consciences also bearing witness, and their thoughts now accusing, now even defending them.) This will take place on the day when God will judge men's secrets through Jesus Christ, as my gospel declares.

Romans 5:1-11

Therefore, since we have been justified through faith, we have peace with God through our Lord Jesus Christ, through whom we have gained access by faith into this grace in which we now stand. And we rejoice in the hope of the glory of God. Not only so, but we also rejoice in our sufferings, because we know that suffering produces perseverance; perseverance, character; and character, hope. And hope does not disappoint us, because God has poured out his love into our hearts by the Holy Spirit, whom he has given us.

You see, at just the right time, when we were still powerless, Christ died for the ungodly. Very rarely will anyone die for a righteous man, though for a good man someone might possibly dare to die. But God demonstrates his own love for us in this: While we were still sinners, Christ died for us.

Since we have now been justified by his blood, how much more shall we be saved from God's wrath through him! For if, when we were God's enemies, we were reconciled to him through the death of his Son, how much more, having been reconciled, shall we be saved through his life! Not only is this so, but we also rejoice in God through our Lord Jesus Christ, through whom we have now received reconciliation.

Romans 8:14-23

Those who are led by the Spirit of God are sons of God. For you did not receive a spirit that makes you a slave again to fear, but you received the Spirit of sonship. And by him we cry, "Abba, Father." The Spirit himself testifies with our spirit that we are God's children. Now if we are children, then we are heirs—heirs of God and co-heirs with Christ, if indeed we share in his sufferings in order that we may also share in his glory.

I consider that our present sufferings are not worth comparing with the glory that will be revealed in us. The creation waits in eager expectation for the sons of God to be revealed. For the creation was subjected to frustration, not by its own choice, but by the will of the one who subjected it, in hope that the creation itself will be liberated from its bondage to decay and brought into the glorious freedom of the children of God.

We know that the whole creation has been groaning as in the pains of childbirth right up to the present time. Not only so, but we ourselves, who have the firstfruits of the Spirit, groan inwardly as we wait eagerly for our adoption as sons, the redemption of our bodies.

Romans 8:31-35, 37-39

If God is for us, who can be against us? He who did not spare his own Son, but gave him up for us all—how will he not also, along with him, graciously give us all things? Who will bring any charge against those whom God has chosen? It is God who justifies. Who is he that condemns? Christ Jesus, who died—more than that, who was raised to life—is at the right hand of God and is also interceding for us. Who shall separate us from the love of Christ? Shall trouble or hardship or persecution or famine or nakedness or danger or sword?

No, in all these things we are more than conquerors through him who loved us. For I am convinced that neither death nor life, neither angels nor demons, neither the present nor the future, nor any powers, neither height nor depth, nor anything else in all creation, will be able to separate us from the love of God that is in Christ Jesus our Lord.

Romans 14:7-9, 10-12 [appropriate for those whose faith is unknown]

For none of us lives to himself alone and none of us dies to himself alone. If we live, we live to the Lord; and if we die, we die to the Lord. So, whether we live or die, we belong to the Lord.

For this very reason, Christ died and returned to life so that he might be the Lord of both the dead and the living.

We will all stand before God's judgment seat. It is written: "'As surely as I live,' says the Lord, 'every knee will bow before me; every tongue will confess to God.'" So then, each of us will give an account of himself to God.

1 Corinthians 15:20-28 (or use 20-23)

But Christ has indeed been raised from the dead, the firstfruits of those who have fallen asleep. For since death came through a man, the resurrection of the dead comes also through a man. For as in Adam all die, so in Christ all will be made alive. But each in his own turn: Christ, the firstfruits; then, when he comes, those who belong to him. [Then the end will come, when he hands over the kingdom to God the Father after he has destroyed all dominion, authority and power. For he must reign until he has put all his enemies under his feet. The last enemy to be destroyed is death. For he "has put everything under his feet." Now when it says that "everything" has been put under him, it is clear that this does not include God himself, who put everything under Christ. When he has done this, then the Son himself will be made subject to him who put everything under him, so that God may be all in all.]

1 Corinthians 15:50-57

I declare to you, brothers, that flesh and blood cannot inherit the kingdom of God, nor does the perishable inherit the imperishable. Listen, I tell you a mystery: We will not all sleep, but we will all be changed—in a flash, in the twinkling of an eye, at the last trumpet. For the trumpet will sound, the dead will be raised imperishable, and we will be changed. For the perishable must clothe itself with the imperishable, and the mortal with immortality. When the perishable has been clothed with the imperishable, and the mortal with immortality, then the saying that is written will come true: "Death has been swallowed up in victory."

"Where, O death, is your victory?
Where, O death, is your sting?"

The sting of death is sin, and the power of sin is the law. But thanks be to God! He gives us the victory through our Lord Jesus Christ.

2 Corinthians 4:7-18 (or use 7-11, 16-18)

But we have this treasure in jars of clay to show that this all-surpassing power is from God and not from us. We are hard pressed on every side, but not crushed; perplexed, but not in despair; persecuted, but not abandoned; struck down, but not destroyed. We always carry around in our body the death of Jesus, so that the life of Jesus may also be revealed in our body. For we who are alive are always being given over to death for Jesus' sake, so that his life may be revealed in our mortal body. [So then, death is at work in us, but life is at work in you.

It is written: "I believed; therefore I have spoken." With that same spirit of faith we also believe and therefore speak, because we know that the one who raised the Lord Jesus from the dead will also raise us with Jesus and present us with you in his presence. All this is for your benefit, so that the grace that is reaching more and more people may cause thanksgiving to overflow to the glory of God.]

Therefore we do not lose heart. Though outwardly we are wasting away, yet inwardly we are being renewed day by day. For our light and momentary troubles are achieving for us an eternal glory that far outweighs them all. So we fix our eyes not on what is seen, but on what is unseen. For what is seen is temporary, but what is unseen is eternal.

2 Corinthians 5:1-10 (or use 1, 6-10)

Now we know that if the earthly tent we live in is destroyed, we have a building from God, an eternal house in heaven, not built by human hands. [Meanwhile we groan, longing to be clothed with our heavenly dwelling, because when we are clothed, we will not be found naked. For while we are in this tent, we groan and are burdened, because we do not wish to be unclothed but to be clothed with our heavenly dwelling, so that what is mortal may be swallowed up by life. Now it is God who has made us for this very purpose and has given us the Spirit as a deposit, guaranteeing what is to come.]

Therefore we are always confident and know that as long as we are at home in the body we are away from the Lord. We live by faith, not by sight. We are confident, I say, and would prefer to be away from the body and at home with the Lord. So we make it our goal to please him, whether we are at home in the body or away from it. For we must all appear before the judgment seat of Christ, that each one may receive what is due him for the things done while in the body, whether good or bad.

Philippians 3:20-21

But our citizenship is in heaven. And we eagerly await a Savior from there, the Lord Jesus Christ, who, by the power that enables him to bring everything under his control, will transform our lowly bodies so that they will be like his glorious body.

Colossians 2:9-12

For in Christ all the fullness of the Deity lives in bodily form, and you have been given fullness in Christ, who is the head over every power and authority. In him you were also circumcised, in the putting off of the sinful nature, not with a circumcision done by the hands of men but with the circumcision done by Christ, having been buried with him in baptism and raised with him through your faith in the power of God, who raised him from the dead.

1 Thessalonians 4:13-18

Brothers, we do not want you to be ignorant about those who fall asleep, or to grieve like the rest of men, who have no hope. We believe that Jesus died and rose again and so we believe that God will bring with Jesus those who have fallen asleep in him. According to the Lord's own word, we tell you that we who are still alive, who are left till the coming of the Lord, will certainly not precede those who have fallen asleep. For the Lord himself will come down from heaven, with a loud command, with the voice of the archangel and with the trumpet call of God, and the dead in Christ will rise first. After that, we who are still alive and are left will be caught up together with them in the clouds to meet the Lord in the air. And so we will be with the Lord forever. Therefore encourage each other with these words.

2 Timothy 2:8-13

Remember Jesus Christ, raised from the dead, descended from David. This is my gospel, for which I am suffering even to the point of being chained like a criminal. But God's word is not chained. Therefore I endure everything for the sake of the elect, that they too may obtain the salvation that is in Christ Jesus, with eternal glory. Here is a trustworthy saying:

If we died with him,
    we will also live with him;
if we endure,
    we will also reign with him.
If we disown him,
    he will also disown us;
if we are faithless,
    he will remain faithful,
    for he cannot disown himself.

2 Timothy 4:6-8

For I am already being poured out like a drink offering, and the time has come for my departure. I have fought the good fight, I have finished the race, I have kept the faith. Now there is in store for me the crown of righteousness, which the Lord, the righteous Judge, will award to me on that day—and not only to me, but also to all who have longed for his appearing.

Hebrews 11:1-3, 6-7, 12-16, 12:1-2

Now faith is being sure of what we hope for and certain of what we do not see. This is what the ancients were commended for.

By faith we understand that the universe was formed at God's command, so that what is seen was not made out of what was visible.

All these people were still living by faith when they died. They did not receive the things promised; they only saw them and welcomed them from a distance. And they admitted that they were aliens and strangers on earth. People who say such things show that they are looking for a country of their own. If they had been thinking of the country they had left, they would have had opportunity to return. Instead, they were longing for a better country—a heavenly one. Therefore God is not ashamed to be called their God, for he has prepared a city for them.

Therefore, since we are surrounded by such a great cloud of witnesses, let us throw off everything that hinders and the sin that so easily entangles, and let us run with perseverance the race marked out for us. Let us fix our eyes on Jesus, the author and perfecter of our faith, who for the joy set before him endured the cross, scorning its shame, and sat down at the right hand of the throne of God.

1 Peter 1:3-9

Praise be to the God and Father of our Lord Jesus Christ! In his great mercy he has given us new birth into a living hope through the resurrection of Jesus Christ from the dead, and into an inheritance that can never perish, spoil or fade—kept in heaven for you, who through faith are shielded by God's power until the coming of the salvation that is ready to be revealed in the last time. In this you greatly rejoice, though now for a little while you may have had to suffer grief in all kinds of trials. These have come so that your faith—of greater worth than gold, which perishes even though refined by fire—may be proved genuine and may result in praise, glory and honor when Jesus Christ is revealed. Though you have not seen him, you love him; and even though you do not see him now, you believe in him and are filled with an inexpressible and glorious joy, for you are receiving the goal of your faith, the salvation of your souls.

1 John 3:1-3

How great is the love the Father has lavished on us, that we should be called children of God! And that is what we are! The reason the world does not know us is that it did not know him. Dear friends, now we are children of God, and what we will be has not yet been made known. But we know that when he appears, we shall be like him, for we shall see him as he is. Everyone who has this hope in him purifies himself, just as he is pure.

Revelation 14:1-3, 6-7, 12-13

Then I looked, and there before me was the Lamb, standing on Mount Zion, and with him 144,000 who had his name and his Father's name written on their foreheads. And I heard a sound from heaven like the roar of rushing waters and like a loud peal of thunder. The sound I heard was like that of harpists playing their harps. And they sang a new song before the throne and before the four living creatures and the elders. No one could learn the song except the 144,000 who had been redeemed from the earth.

Then I saw another angel flying in midair, and he had the eternal gospel to proclaim to those who live on the earth—to every nation, tribe, language and people. He said in a loud voice, "Fear God and give him glory, because the hour of his judgment has come. Worship him who made the heavens, the earth, the sea and the springs of water."

This calls for patient endurance on the part of the saints who obey God's commandments and remain faithful to Jesus.

Then I heard a voice from heaven say, "Write: Blessed are the dead who die in the Lord from now on."

"Yes," says the Spirit, "they will rest from their labor, for their deeds will follow them."

Revelation 20:11-21:1

Then I saw a great white throne and him who was seated on it. Earth and sky fled from his presence, and there was no place for them. And I saw the dead, great and small, standing before the throne, and books were opened. Another book was opened, which is the book of life. The dead were judged according to what they had done as recorded in the books. The sea gave up the dead that were in it, and death and Hades gave up the dead that were in them, and each person was judged according to what he had done. Then death and Hades were thrown into the lake of fire. The lake of fire is the second death. If anyone's name was not found written in the book of life, he was thrown into the lake of fire. Then I saw a new heaven and a new earth, for the first heaven and the first earth had passed away, and there was no longer any sea.

Revelation 21:1-5, 6-7

Then I saw a new heaven and a new earth, for the first heaven and the first earth had passed away, and there was no longer any sea. I saw the Holy City, the new Jerusalem, coming down out of heaven from God, prepared as a bride beautifully dressed for her husband. And I heard a loud voice from the throne saying, "Now the dwelling of God is with men, and he will live with them. They will be his people, and God himself will be with them and be their God. He will wipe every tear from their eyes. There will be no more death or mourning or crying or pain, for the old order of things has passed away."

He who was seated on the throne said, “I am making everything new!”

“To him who is thirsty I will give to drink without cost from the spring of the water of life. He who overcomes will inherit all this, and I will be his God and he will be my son.”

Confessions and Liturgical Texts

The following excerpts from Scripture and from several confessions and liturgical texts may be used, as indicated, in the Funeral or Committal services.

The Apostles' Creed

*[The Apostles' Creed may be spoken or sung by the congregation (*Psalter Hymnal *518, 519).]*

I believe in God, the Father Almighty,
creator of heaven and earth.

I believe in Jesus Christ, his only Son, our Lord,
who was conceived by the Holy Spirit
and born of the Virgin Mary.
He suffered under Pontius Pilate,
was crucified, died, and was buried;
he descended to hell.
The third day he rose again from the dead.
He ascended to heaven
and is seated at the right hand of God the Father almighty.
From there he will come to judge the living and the dead.

I believe in the Holy Spirit,
the holy catholic church,
the communion of saints,
the forgiveness of sins,
the resurrection of the body,
and the life everlasting. Amen.

The Nicene Creed

[The Nicene Creed may be spoken or sung by the congregation (Psalter Hymnal *520).]*

We believe in one God,
the Father almighty,
maker of heaven and earth,
of all things visible and invisible.

And in one Lord Jesus Christ,
the only Son of God,
begotten from the Father before all ages,
God from God,
Light from Light,
true God from true God,
begotten, not made;
of the same essence as the Father.
Through him all things were made.
For us and for our salvation
he came down from heaven;
he became incarnate by the Holy Spirit and the Virgin Mary,
and was made human.
He was crucified for us under Pontius Pilate;
he suffered and was buried.
The third day he rose again, according to the Scriptures.
He ascended to heaven
and is seated at the right hand of the Father.
He will come again with glory
to judge the living and the dead.
His kingdom will never end.

And we believe in the Holy Spirit,
the Lord, the giver of life.
He proceeds from the Father and the Son,
and with the Father and the Son is worshiped and glorified.
He spoke through the prophets.
We believe in one holy catholic and apostolic church.

We affirm one baptism for the forgiveness of sins.
We look forward to the resurrection of the dead,
and to life in the world to come. Amen.

The Heidelberg Catechism

Question and Answer 1

**Q. What is your only comfort
in life and in death?**

A. That I am not my own,
but belong—
body and soul,
in life and in death—
to my faithful Savior Jesus Christ.

He has fully paid for all my sins with his precious blood,
and has set me free from the tyranny of the devil.
He also watches over me in such a way
that not a hair can fall from my head
without the will of my Father in heaven:
in fact, all things must work together for my salvation.

Because I belong to him,
Christ, by his Holy Spirit,
assures me of eternal life
and makes me wholeheartedly willing and ready
from now on to live for him.

Question and Answer 52

**Q. How does Christ's return
"to judge the living and the dead"
comfort you?**

A. In all my distress and persecution
I turn my eyes to the heavens
and confidently await as judge the very One

who has already stood trial in my place before God
and so has removed the whole curse from me.
All his enemies and mine
he will condemn to everlasting punishment:
but me and all his chosen ones
he will take along with him
into the joy and glory of heaven.

Question and Answer 57

Q. How does "the resurrection of the body" comfort you?

A. Not only my soul
will be taken immediately after this life
to Christ its head,
but even my very flesh, raised by the power of Christ,
will be reunited with my soul
and made like Christ's glorious body.

Question and Answer 58

Q. How does the article concerning "life everlasting" comfort you?

A. Even as I already now
experience in my heart
the beginning of eternal joy,
so after this life I will have
perfect blessedness such as
no eye has seen,
no ear has heard,
no human heart has ever imagined:
a blessedness in which to praise God eternally.

Other Liturgical Resources

Our World Belongs to God

[Stanzas 56-58, abbreviated]

Our hope for a new earth is not tied
to what humans can do,
for we believe that one day
every challenge to God's rule
and every resistance to his will shall be crushed.
Then his kingdom shall come fully,
and our Lord shall rule forever.

We long for that day
when Jesus will return as triumphant king,
when the dead will be raised
and all people will stand before his judgement.
We face that day without fear,
for the Judge is our Savior.
Our daily lives of service aim for the moment
when the Son will present his people to the Father.
Then God will be shown to be true, holy, and gracious.
All who have been on the Lord's side
will be honored,
the fruit of even small acts of
obedience will be displayed.

With the whole creation
we wait for the purifying fire of judgement.
For then we will see the Lord face to face.
He will heal our hurts,
end our wars,
and make the crooked straight.
Then we will join in the new song
to the Lamb without blemish
who made us a kingdom and priests.

God will be all in all,
righteousness and peace will flourish,
everything will be made new,
and every eye will see at last
that our world belongs to God!
Hallelujah! Come, Lord Jesus.

Te Deum (You are God)

[An ancient liturgical affirmation of faith. The Te Deum *may be spoken or sung by the congregation (*Psalter Hymnal *504).]*

You are God: we praise you;
You are the Lord: we acclaim you;
You are the eternal Father:
All creation worships you.
To you all angels, all the powers of heaven,
Cherubim and Seraphim, sing in endless praise:
Holy, holy, holy Lord, God of power and might,
heaven and earth are full of your glory.
The glorious company of apostles praise you.
The noble fellowship of prophets praise you.
The white-robed army of martyrs praise you.
Throughout the world the holy church acclaims you;
Father, of majesty unbounded,
your true and only Son, worthy of all worship,
and the Holy Spirit, advocate and guide.

You, Christ, are the King of glory,
the eternal Son of the Father.
When you became human to set us free
you did not spurn the Virgin's womb.
You overcame the sting of death,
and opened the kingdom of heaven to all believers.
You are seated at God's right hand in glory.
We believe that you will come and be our judge.

Come, then, Lord, and help your people,
bought with the price of your own blood,
and bring us with your saints to glory everlasting.

Romans 8:35, 37-39 (altered)

Leader: Who shall separate us from the love of Christ?
Shall tribulation or distress?
Or persecution or famine?
Or nakedness or danger or sword?

People: No, in all these things we are more than conquerors
through him who loved us.
For we are sure that neither death, nor life,
nor angels, nor demons,
nor the present, nor the future,
nor powers, nor height, nor depth,
nor anything else in all creation,
will be able to separate us from the love of God
that is in Christ Jesus our Lord. Amen.

Affirmation of Faith

This is the good news which we have received,
in which we stand,
and by which we are saved,
if we hold it fast:
that Christ died for our sins according to the Scriptures,
that he was buried,
that he was raised on the third day,
and that he appeared first to the women,
then to Peter, and to the Twelve,
and then to many faithful witnesses. *1 Corinthians 15:1-6*

We believe that Jesus is the Christ, *Mark 16:9 (1-9)*
the Son of the living God. *Matthew 16:16*
Jesus Christ is the first and the last, *Revelation 22:13*
the beginning and the end;
he is our Lord and our God. Amen. *John 20:28*

—*TF*

Prayers for Special Circumstances

The following additional prayers are provided for use in unique circumstances and situations. They may be used in conjunction with the other prayers found in any of the services or at any point they are deemed appropriate.

[For one who died suddenly]

O God, you search our hearts and know us through and through.
Wherever we are, no matter how near or far,
you are there.
However we think or feel, no matter how high or low,
you know and understand.
In our grief and shock,
our minds are a tangled mass of conflicting thoughts,
and our hearts are overwhelmed with pain.
We ask questions for which there seem to be no answers.
We experience grief for which there seems to be no consolation.
O God, we are hurt so deeply, it seems beyond words.
All we need, all we ask, in this dark moment
is that you hold us close, and not let us go.
Embrace us and love us, Lord, even in our terrible pain,
for somehow we know that in your embrace
healing will finally come.
Somehow we know that in your care
our broken hearts will know a gentle mending.
Through Jesus Christ our Lord.
AMEN.

[or]

Why, Lord, must evil seem to get its way?
We do confess that our sin is deeply shameful;
but now the wicked are openly scornful—
they mock your name and laugh at our dismay.
We know your providential love holds true:
nothing can curse us endlessly with sorrow.
Transform, dear Lord, this damage into good;
show us your glory, hidden by this evil.

Why, Lord, did you abruptly take him/her home?
Could you not wait to summon him/her before you?
Why must we feel the sting of death's old cruelty?
Come quickly, Lord, do not leave us alone.
We plead: Repair the brokenness we share.
Chastise no more lest it destroy your creatures.
Hear this lament as intercessory prayer,
and speak your powerful word to make us hopeful.

Why, Lord, must any child of yours be hurt?
Does all our pain and sorrow somehow please you?
You are a God so jealous for our praises—
hear this lament as prayer that fills the earth.
We plead: Repair the brokenness we share.
Chastise no more lest it destroy your creatures.
Hear this lament as intercessory prayer,
and speak your powerful word to make us hopeful.
AMEN.

—PsH

[For one who died an untimely death]

Leader: Gentle God,
comfort us in our loss.
Our tears are real;
they are tears of sorrow.
Stand by us as we cry out to you.

People: Loving God, comfort us;
embrace us in our grieving.

Leader: Beloved Creator,
we give you thanks for your love.

When we stand before birth and new life,
such praise arises swiftly from within us
and slips easily from our tongues.

But when we find ourselves, as we do now,
encircled by death and loss,
gratitude and blessing choke in our hearts
as tears cloud our eyes
and sorrow makes confusion of understanding.

Gentle God, even as we stand in the shadow of your love,
we feel more in a place of shadows,
lacking light and warmth,
than in a place of love.

People: Loving God, comfort us;
embrace us in our grieving.

Leader: Death has left us confused and sorrowful,
filling us with questions
that are as deeply mysterious as the oceans
and as unanswerable as the language of the stars.

These are not easy questions,
but ones of anger and grief.

Their taste is as bitter as gall,
their touch burns into our souls.

Like Mary and John, our questions are as dark
as those clouds that hung over the cross.

Like countless others
who have stood in the wake of death,
we have questions that throw us into the same despair
as the absence we now feel.

We join a multitude of others before us
who have wrestled with the "why" of painful loss
and the "where" of your caring presence.

People: Loving God, comfort us;
embrace us in our grieving.

Leader: Help us, God, to realize
that we are not alone in our sorrow,
but mix our tears with yours.

You who embraced a crucified Son
feel deeply the pain of this broken and battered world.
Keep vigil with us now.

People: Loving God, comfort us;
embrace us in our grieving.

Leader: Tender God, accept our desperate heart,
filled with deepest sorrow.

As the emptiness of loss becomes
a cruel and heavy burden to carry,
help us to lighten the load.

As despair and anger become merciless taskmasters,
help us to ease our slavery.

As fear floods our waking and sleeping hours,
help us to find the peace of faith.

People: Loving God, comfort us;
embrace us in our grieving.

Leader: Creator, grant us the courage
to journey through our grieving and our pain.

Grant us the faith to know
that tombs are not the last word
but that resurrection awaits us all.

In these dark times, send your Spirit
to heal our sadness and our anger
so that, like Christ,
we may begin to heal one another.

People: Loving God, comfort us;
embrace us in our grieving.

—CGP

[After the death of an infant or child]

O Merciful God,
we thank you for the love that cares for us in life
and watches over us in death.
May we, in faith and hope,
give back to you the life which was given to us in love.
We thank you for our Savior's joy in little children
and for the assurance that to such belongs the kingdom of heaven.
We believe that in death, as in life,
__________ is *(they are)* in his holy keeping.

In our sorrow
make us strong to commit ourselves, and those we love,
to your never-failing care.
In our perplexity
may we trust where we cannot understand.
In our loneliness
may we remember __________ *(this child)*
with love and thanksgiving,
trusting that you will keep him/her in your loving arms
until the morning breaks and the shadows flee away,
through Jesus Christ our Lord.
AMEN.

—TF

[or]

Blessed Jesus, lover of children,
with broken hearts we cry to you for help.
With great joy and anticipation
we awaited this beloved child,
and now we have been brought low by his/her death.
Our pain is nearly inexpressible,
but we know you weep with us in our loss.
Heal our grief, fill the void within,
and help us, in the midst of groaning sorrow,
to hear your voice of comfort and grace,
through Jesus Christ our Lord.
AMEN.

—*TF*

[After the death of a young person]

Lord God, source and destiny of our lives,
in your loving providence you gave us __________
to grow in wisdom, stature, and grace.
Now he/she is gone,
and we grieve the loss of one so young,
groping for understanding and meaning.
Father, as he/she grew toward maturity,
we sensed the exciting promise of what was to come.
But now that promise seems betrayed by death,
and our hopes and dreams for __________
lie shattered before the grave.
Comfort us, O God,
for you conquered even death and the grave.

Give us grace to see him/her with the eyes of faith,
in the full stature of Christ,
standing with all the saints and angels
in perfect wholeness and dazzling glory.
Through Jesus Christ our Lord.
AMEN.

[After the death of an aged parent]

God of our ancestors in faith,
by the covenant you made with your people
you taught us to strengthen the bonds of family
through faith, honor, and love.
As we honored this our mother/father in life,
so we honor him/her in death.
As he/she has joined that one great family of God,
may our faith now expand to grasp
your loving purpose to gather all your children
from the ends of the earth,
into the joy of your everlasting kingdom;
through Jesus Christ our Lord.
AMEN.

[After the death of a husband or wife]

Eternal God,
you made the union of man and woman
a sign of the bond between Christ and the church.
Grant mercy and peace to __________,
who was united in love with his/her husband/wife.
May the care and devotion of his/her life on earth
find a lasting reward in heaven.
Look kindly on his/her husband/wife and family/children
as now they turn to your compassion and love.
Strengthen his/her/their faith
and lighten his/her/their loss;
We ask this through Christ our Lord.

—OCF

[After the death of an elderly person]

God of endless ages,
from one generation to the next
you have been our refuge and strength.
Before the mountains were born
or earth came to be,
you are God.

We give you thanks for _________,
and for his/her long life of humble service

[here particular remembrance may be made of his/her unique qualities of life and service].

We rejoice that now, by your mercy,
_________ has now laid down his/her earthly burdens
and has joined the company of the redeemed in glory;
through Jesus Christ our Lord.
AMEN.

[For one who died after a long illness]

God of deliverance and mercy,
_________, our brother/sister,
knew the cross of weakness and pain.
Even in great suffering
he/she placed *(struggled to place)* his/her trust in you alone.
We thank you that now his/her suffering is ended,
and the night of pain is transformed
in the dazzling dawn of your presence.
Through Jesus Christ our Lord.
AMEN.

[For one who died suddenly and/or violently]

Eternal God,
In all life's changes and uncertainties,
you are with us through every step of our journey.

We are stunned by the sudden *(and violent)* death
of _________, our brother/sister.
Lead us from numbing shock
through the painful stab of reality
to the comfort of your never-failing peace.
Help us to gather our shattered lives together again
and find the strength to go on
in the hope of the resurrection.
May we find peace in the assurance that
nothing can separate us from your love
in Jesus Christ our Lord.
AMEN.

[For one who died by suicide]

Dear God, lover of your people,
you hold dear all you have made.
You understand our terrible fears,
our deep depressions, our hopeless moments.

Our lives, too, are shattered
by this terrible act.
Gentle Shepherd, lead us to peace, forgiveness, and hope.
Deliver us from guilt and bitterness,
and heal our broken hearts.
Help us to see beyond both his/her pain, and our own
to the wholeness of your kingdom
when we shall all gather in your presence,
and every tear will be wiped away,
and every wrong made right;
through Jesus Christ our Lord.
AMEN.

[For one of poor reputation who lived an openly sinful life]

God of all mercies,
all of us stand condemned before you,
but for the grace of Christ our Lord.
We place in your merciful hands __________, our brother/sister.
His/her life was filled with sin and struggle,
but only you, all-knowing and merciful God,
perceive what mustard seed of faith and hope
was hidden in his/her heart.
Only you know to what measure he/she
was sinned against as well as sinning.
Lord Jesus Christ, you who welcomed the thief into paradise,
have mercy on us all.
AMEN.

[For one who was a victim of murder]

Eternal God and judge of all the earth,
we turn to you in our time of outraged sorrow.
Comfort us, upon whom this great tragedy has come.
Sustain us who mourn this innocent victim,
torn away from family and friends so suddenly and violently.
O God, you have said, "Vengeance is mine, I will repay."
Deliver us from bitterness, hatred, and the desire for revenge.
Give us the grace to pray even for the murderer,
and, in the healing of time, to forgive
even as our Lord forgave his murderers.
We trust in you, O Lord, to lighten our darkness
and bring us out of this time of shock and anguish.
Grant that we may see with the eyes of faith
that nothing can separate us, or anyone in your hands,
from your love;
through Jesus Christ our Lord.
AMEN.

[For one who was not known to be a Christian]

Loving and merciful God,
you search our hearts and know us through and through.
We commend __________, our brother/sister,
to your merciful care,
knowing that you, judge of all the earth, will do right.
We thank you for all in him/her that was right and good

[here certain virtues of life and character may be remembered].

Comfort us now, God of all grace,
and teach us all to number our days
that we may grow in wisdom and in faith.
May this sobering encounter with death stir us all
to seek eternal life through your Son,
our Lord Jesus Christ.
AMEN.

Music for the Funeral

LeRoy G. Christoffels

In a funeral, as in any service of worship, well-chosen music can aid the sorrowing community to lift their hearts to the God of all comfort. Psalms and hymns are communal sung prayers. The community of mourners unites in song to express its sorrow and grief to the Man of Sorrows, and to rejoice in the gift of the life from the One who has died. In song the mourners express together the faith that is the foundation of their recovery and renewal in hopeful living.

The prayer song of the sorrowing may begin with a plaintive "I cried out to God to help me: in distress and sorrow, hear me" (*PsH* 77:1) and crescendo to "By the sea of crystal, saints in glory stand" (*PsH* 620:1). Following the singing of "Precious to God the dying of his saints" (*PsH* 116:5) with "Ten thousand times ten thousand give glory to the Lamb" (*PsH* 619:1) can stir sorrowing hearts to hope.

In developing the funeral service, the pastor, musicians, and family should be guided by appropriate principles that have well-considered implications for the service. Those who plan the funeral together can find a helpful statement of principle for church music adopted by the Christian Reformed Church in 1979 (included in the Introduction to the 1987 edition of the *Psalter Hymnal*).

> The music of the church should be appropriate for worship—that is, it should be liturgical and have aesthetic integrity. The music of worship should serve the dialogue between God and his people.
>
> —*Psalter Hymnal* 1987, p. 11

Especially when the funeral service is held in the church building, the awareness of being part of a body of believers gives us reason to consider the value of this basic principle. The guidelines and suggestions for funeral music that follow are rooted in that principle.

1. Express both grief and hope.

There are two purposes for music at a funeral. Both must be present, though the emphasis on one or the other will depend on the situation. First, we need to communally express the reality of the loss, grief, and pain that we feel at the death of the loved one before the God who sees and hears our grief. Second, we need to express the hope of believers in the equally great reality of eternal life and God's coming kingdom. We need to lift the hearts of the mourners to the clear message of this hope, even when it appears that the one who has died was not a believer.

When the pastor and others who plan the service keep these two purposes clearly in mind, they will be able to choose music that helps the grieving family and community to look above the present hour to the eternal God. Both of these purposes are beautifully met, for example, in Henry F. Lyte's familiar "Abide with Me" (*PsH* 442), where the constant presence of the Lord is discovered precisely in our grief. And Georg Neumark's "If You But Trust in God to Guide You" (*PsH* 446) recognizes our need and our uncertainty, and directs us to the changeless love of God.

2. Make sure corporate music predominates.

Priority is given to congregational worship in regular corporate worship, and that principle is beneficial for the funeral as well. Pastors who appreciate the value of experiencing and expressing grief as a believing *community* will encourage congregational singing. Great comfort can be gained from the entire congregation singing the church's hymns and psalms. Music and song may be included wherever possible in the various gatherings surrounding the funeral: at the funeral home, in the committal service, and even during the customary fellowship hour following the service.

3. Focus on God.

Music at a funeral is most helpful when its focus is on God rather than on ourselves. The sorrowing heart needs the assurance that rests in knowing God's sovereign grace, constant covenant keeping, and rich knowledge of his people. "Great Is Thy Faithfulness" and "How Great Thou Art" are two favorite hymns, precisely because they offer this genuine hope and comfort.

4. Balance family choices with the considerations of the larger community.

Often family members will select songs that were treasured by the deceased person in life. While using favorites can be an excellent place to start, a word of caution is in order: not all of those songs may really offer needed comfort or direct the hearts of the mourners to God. These songs may be only vaguely related to our present experience of both sorrow and hope.

Hymns or anthems that truly comfort us and assist us in grieving lift us up from genuine depths to true and specific realities. Family and personal choices should be complemented by the communal songs of the church, which reside primarily in the pew hymnal. Respect the choices of the family, but surround them with the song of the church of all ages.

5. Involve the choir.

If a choir regularly participates in congregational worship, they should be encouraged, if possible, to gather also for a funeral service. A choral offering of song provides a gift from the congregation to the grieving family and community. The choir need not sing an elaborate anthem; singing one stanza of a congregational hymn may be very appropriate. For example,

"Praise, My Soul, the King of Heaven" (*PsH* 475) may be sung with the choir only on the second stanza.

If a choir will be participating, those responsible for planning the service need to recognize that choir rehearsal and preparation requires special coordination. And because of demands of work and other activities, planners should understand that the time of the service may have to be adjusted to permit a good balance of singers to be present (late afternoons or evenings may be more convenient for a larger number of singers). While coordination is less complicated for a small ensemble or a solo, the choir better emphasizes the corporate nature of the assembly. Soloists or groups of singers should be aware that they are expressing not merely their own feelings; they are expressing the praise and prayer of the assembled community.

6. Plan for the acoustical setting.

Acoustics should not be forgotten in the process of planning the musical aspects of the service. Usually the acoustics are much better in the church than in the funeral home (one of many reasons commending the church as the place for the funeral). When the service is held in the funeral home, carpet and other sound-absorbing decoration may pose special obstacles for singing. Instruments may not be adequate for supporting congregational singing or for accompanying a choir or soloist.

But even if the acoustical setting is poor, the community gathered should sing. Recorded music should be discouraged as a substitute for singing; grief and hope should arise from those present. The worshiper must be able to offer up genuine prayer and crying to God.

7. Lead with strength and confidence.

In a context of the denial of death and its reality, it's not surprising that we usually assume funeral music should be soft, slow-moving, and weak-sounding, and that triumphant sounds are inappropriate. The Christian reality is that while death is the last enemy, through Christ it is no longer a powerful enemy. Death marks the believer's entrance into eternal life. So while the pain and loss of those left behind are real, the triumphant home-going of the deceased should also be reflected in the way music is used. Mourners do not benefit from weak and indecisive singing or accompaniment. They are seeking firm and confident assurance.

At the Christian funeral, psalms and hymns are not sung to cover up the pain or to distract the sorrowing from death's reality. The style of playing and singing we use for each hymn or psalm should be appropriate to its content and setting. Triumphant hymns should be played and sung in the spirit in which they were composed. For example, Genevan Psalm 68:1 and 6, which includes the words "Give praise to God with reverence deep; he daily comes our lives to keep" should demonstrate the vigorous praise and sturdy confidence which both text and tune imply. "O God, Our Help in Ages Past" should never become a dirge. When praising God for the life and gifts of the person who has been taken, or for the confidence we have in God's enduring promises, let both organ and congregation play and sing appropriately. Even hymns or spirituals that directly express grief should not lack strength or confidence.

The following groups of psalms and hymns are suggestions for the funeral service. Most hymnals have listings of appropriate songs in the topical index; the list below includes and expands on the list under the entry "Funerals" in the 1987 *Psalter Hymnal.*

In most funeral services, there will be a progression in hymns that moves from grief and pain to hope and triumph. The psalms, hymns, and Bible songs listed here are arranged in three general categories reflecting this progression.

Songs Expressing Sorrow and Grief (though never without Christian hope)

Psalm 17	"LORD, Listen to My Righteous Plea"
Psalm 39	"Once I Said, 'I Must Keep Quiet'"
Psalm 42	"As a Deer in Want of Water"
Psalm 43	"Defend Me, LORD, from Those Who Charge Me"
Psalm 77	"I Cried Out to God to Help Me"
Psalm 116:3, 5	"I Love the LORD, for He Has Heard My Voice"
Bible Song 217	"Jesus, Remember Me"
Hymn 442	"Abide with Me"
Hymn 491	"Our Lives Are Filled with Sorrows"
Hymn 576:5	"A Congregational Lament"
Hymn 625	"Lord, Listen to Your Children Praying"

Songs Expressing Confidence and Trust

Psalm 23	"The LORD, My Shepherd, Rules My Life"
Psalm 27	"The LORD God Is My Light and My Salvation"
Psalm 46	"God Is Our Refuge and Our Strength"
Psalm 68	"Let God Arise and by His Might"
Psalm 73	"God Loves All the Righteous"
Psalm 84	"How Lovely Is Your House, O LORD"
Psalm 89	"Forever I Will Sing of Your Great Love, O LORD"
Psalm 90	"Lord, You Have Been Our Dwelling Place"
Psalm 91	"Whoever Shelters with the LORD"
Psalm 103	"Come, Praise the LORD, O My Soul"
Psalm 121	"To the Hills I Lift My Eyes"
Bible Song 162	"My Shepherd is the LORD"
Bible Song 170	"O God, Our Help in Ages Past"
Hymn 248	"I Greet My Sure Redeemer"
Hymn 262	"My Faith Looks Up to Thee"
Hymn 371	"Christ, the Life of All the Living"

Hymn 440	"Children of the Heavenly Father"
Hymn 450	"O God, Our Father, We Come"
Hymn 451	"What God Ordains Is Always Right"
Hymn 463	"O Love of God, How Strong and True"
Hymn 493	"Precious Lord, Take My Hand"
Hymn 543	"Guide Me, O My Great Redeemer"
Hymn 550	"My Shepherd Will Supply My Needs"
Hymn 554	"In Sweet Communion, Lord, with You"
Hymn 556	"Great Is Thy Faithfulness"
Hymn 557	"My Jesus, I Love Thee"
Hymn 558	"Lord of All Hopefulness"
Hymn 617	"Swing Low, Sweet Chariot"
Hymn 634	"Father, We Love You"

Songs Expressing the Triumph of God's Redeemed Children

Psalm 46	"God Is Our Refuge and Our Strength"
Psalm 68:6-9	"Give Praise to God with Reverence Deep"
Psalm 73	"God Loves All the Righteous"
Psalm 89	"Forever I Will Sing of Your Great Love, O LORD"
Psalm 116	"I Love the LORD, for He Has Heard My Voice"
Bible Song 152	"I Will Sing unto the LORD"
Bible Song 161	"The LORD's My Shepherd"
Bible Song 202	"Song of Jonah"
Hymn 239	"Amid the Thronging Worshipers"
Hymn 248	"I Greet My Sure Redeemer"
Hymn 388	"Christ the Lord Is Risen Today"
Hymn 391	"The Strife Is O'er, the Battle Done"
Hymn 392	"A Sound Rings Out, a Joyful Voice/ Daar juicht een toon"
Hymn 399	"Jesus Lives and So Do We"
Hymn 400	"Praise the Savior, Now and Ever"
Hymn 402	"Alleluia, Alleluia! Give Thanks"
Hymn 403	"This Joyful Eastertide"

Hymn 412	"Jesus Shall Reign"
Hymn 413	"Christ Is Alive! Let Christians Sing"
Hymn 439	"We Come to Thank You, God, by Singing"
Hymn 449	"O Righteous, in the Lord Rejoice"
Hymn 465	"Sing Praise to God Who Reigns Above"
Hymn 475	"Praise, My Soul, the King of Heaven"
Hymn 483	"How Great Thou Art"
Hymn 489	"When Peace like a River"
Hymn 500	"How Firm a Foundation"
Hymn 504	"Holy God, We Praise Your Name"
Hymn 505	"For All the Saints"
Hymn 612	"Lo! He Comes, with Clouds Descending"
Hymn 615	"The King Shall Come When Morning Dawns"
Hymn 618	"Jerusalem the Golden"
Hymn 619	"Ten Thousand Times Ten Thousand"
Hymn 620	"By the Sea of Crystal"
Hymn 621	"The God of Abraham Praise"

The Ministry of the Congregation

The Church Order of the Christian Reformed Church affirms that "funerals are not ecclesiastical but family affairs" (Church Order, Art. 70). This provision has a long and interesting history and has been the subject of debate in the CRC (for example, see THE BANNER, June 18, 1984, and *Reformed Worship* 24, June, 1992). Some have advocated a change in the Church Order, placing funerals under the authority of the church council. Others see great wisdom in the present status of funerals as a family matter. Whatever we may think of this provision of the Church Order, the fact is that congregations are involved in many important ways in supporting the grieving family, helping to plan and carry out the funeral service, and, in many cases, preparing the church building for the funeral and other activities associated with the funeral. The extent of this involvement varies from place to place in the denomination.

Family and friends of the deceased need to make many plans and decisions at the time of a death. Often, because they are so overwhelmed by grief and unfamiliar with the funeral planning process, it can be helpful for the church to provide support and guidance. In the absence of that guidance and support, the family usually only has the guidance of the funeral director, who may or may not be familiar with the particular faith and customs of the family and their church.

However, many councils and congregations are unsure of how to provide such support. Since our Church Order does not provide guidance for funerals, our churches have seldom discussed how funerals and their surrounding customs fit into the life of a congregation and how they can best express the faith and love of the congregation. That is not to say that funeral customs have not evolved over the years. They have, and are often firmly entrenched. But the customs we often unthinkingly follow may not be the best expressions of the faith and life of the congregation.

Councils (while I am using the term council throughout, the consistory may be the appropriate body in a particular congregation) may want to discuss such matters as the merits of having funeral services in the church sanctuary, the use of a pall, the importance of calling upon the minister(s) and elders very soon after the death has occurred, stewardship of finances related to funeral expenses, the appropriateness of various methods of body disposal (cremation, donation, etc.), and plans for the support of the family (meals, prayer chains, etc.).

They may wish to invite a funeral director or directors in the congregation or community to participate in the discussion.

When the council members have come to some conclusions about appropriate Christian funeral practices and have formulated some guidelines, they should share these with the congregation. A letter may be the most appropriate vehicle. Initially it could be sent to all members and thereafter to all new members. Since funerals and related matters may not be of immediate significance to a family or individual in the church, and the letter may be lost or overlooked, a periodic reminder (perhaps in a church newsletter) would be advisable.

It is imperative that the council's letter not lay down "rules" or in any way be perceived by the congregation as taking away their right of planning the funeral and other surrounding practices. The council's purpose is to provide guidance and advice to the congregation and to help the members understand that the whole congregation is willing and able to offer support when they face death in their families.

Below you will find a model letter from a council to a congregation. This letter embodies some of the pastoral advice provided in this manual, but it is not meant to be used as is by every congregation. Each council should discuss the matter with a view to the needs of their particular congregation and its prevalent customs, so that their letter can reflect the local situation.

Dear Congregation,

When death strikes, we are often so overwhelmed by the grief and shock of the moment that we have little time to think through all the arrangements and plans leading up to the funeral. Because many of us do not think about funeral arrangements before death comes, we may face a bewildering array of choices and plans that need to be made at a time when we are least able to properly think them through.

In our tradition, funerals are a family matter, but the church has an important role to fulfill in providing support, prayer, and practical help for the bereaved family or individual. As a council, we have discussed ways in which we can give support and advice to the congregation in matters related to death and funerals. While we do not mean in any way to intrude on your own plans and desires regarding death and the funeral, we want to provide a context in which to encourage you to think about these matters and discuss them with your families and friends. The more we discuss and plan beforehand what to do at the time of death, the less burden we place on our loved ones.

1. When a family member dies, it is appropriate to contact the church leadership immediately so that a pastor can offer immediate support and prayer. If circumstances permit, it is very helpful for this first gathering for prayer and words of comfort from Scripture to take place in the presence of the body at the place of death. Either at this time, or soon afterward, the pastor and the family can begin to plan the funeral and make any other arrangements that might include the pastor.

2. At a funeral, grief and faith, thanksgiving and pleading prayer, God's Word and our words, mingle together in a

powerful and healing way. A funeral service is a celebration of the hope of our resurrection through the resurrection of Jesus Christ, which is signed and sealed to us in our baptism. It is an opportunity to share our grief, weakness, doubts, and even anger together, and to comfort one another in faith and love. It is a time to give thanks to God in remembrance of the life of the person who has died. It is a time for prayer in which we can bring our grief and thanksgiving before the God of all comfort and grace. And finally it is a time to hear the Word of God, which is the foundation of our faith and hope.

Therefore, the church sanctuary is the most appropriate place to gather for a funeral. The church is, after all, home for our congregational family and is therefore a good place to surrender our loved one back into the loving embrace of our Lord. You may want to consider the possibility of having the funeral or memorial service in the evening when it is possible for more congregation members to join with the family and other friends. If you choose to use the church sanctuary, it may be appropriate to have a committal service at the cemetery before the memorial service, or on the day after the funeral.

3. We need to realize that we live in a culture that encourages us to avoid pain and tries to shortcut the process of grieving. Those who study bereavement tell us that many psychological and even physical problems plague those who have not given proper time and attention to their grief. It is important to allow ourselves time and opportunity to express anger, doubt, sorrow, fear—whatever we may be feeling.

And it is important to have times and rituals for such expression. The resurrection comes only after the agony of dying, and we are healed only after we are willing to embrace the pain of death and share it with each other. That is why it is important to say farewell to the body of the person who has died and to schedule times to let others gather with the family to comfort each other. That is also why it may be important, if circumstances permit, to go to the cemetery for a committal service, thus facing the reality of the body's burial (or some equivalent ritual if cremation follows the funeral).

As a council we know that the most agonizing times of grief come after the funeral is over and support has waned. We pledge ourselves to provide you with continuing support and counsel in the months and even years after the death has occurred. We will continue to ask you how you are doing and provide ways in which you can express your grief and receive our prayerful support.

4. It is important for us, the living, to think about our own death and how we want to leave behind for others a witness to our faith. This includes thinking about the hymns, Scripture, and other elements that we might want to have at our own funeral, and writing them down. In this process, however, we need to remember that the funeral is for the family and friends left behind, and that they need to grieve as well as celebrate their faith and hope. Loved ones left behind may also be greatly aided when many of the details of the death and burial, such as casket selection, burial plot, and cost considerations, are dealt with beforehand.

[5. The council may wish to address other matters of local custom, such as services the congregation is willing to provide for the family: prayer support, meals for the family in their home, and a gathering after the funeral or memorial service.]

This all sounds rather somber, yet it is a realistic and faith-filled way to prepare for death. Such preparation is important for each one of us because life is fragile, and the hour of our death is unknown. And when we prepare ourselves and our loved ones for death we find, paradoxically but truly, that we are far better prepared to *live* fully and joyfully.

In Christ's Peace,
The Council

Acknowledgments

Scripture

All Scripture references in this resource, unless otherwise indicated, are taken from the HOLY BIBLE, NEW INTERNATIONAL VERSION, copyright © 1973, 1978, 1984 International Bible Society. Used by permission of Zondervan Bible Publishers.

Key to Sources of Prayers and Readings

All prayers not credited were written by Leonard J. Vander Zee. All other prayers were reprinted or adapted from a variety of sources, indicated by initials following the prayers, and are used by permission.

ASB *The Alternative Service Book* 1980. London: © The Central Board of Finance of the Church of England.

BCP *The Book of Common Prayer.* New York: The Church Hymnal Corporation and the Seabury Press, © 1979.

BS *The Book of Services.* Nashville, TN: The United Methodist Publishing House, © 1985.

CGP *Canticles and Gathering Prayers.* Prayers compiled by John P. Mossi, songs by Suzanne Toolan. Winona, MN: The St. Mary's Press, © 1989.

KJV *Holy Bible: King James Version.*

LBW *Lutheran Book of Worship.* Minneapolis, MN: Augsburg Fortress, © 1978.

OCF *Order of Christian Funerals.* Collegeville, MN: International Commission on English in the Liturgy, © 1985.

OS *Occasional Services.* Minneapolis, MN: Augsburg Fortress, © 1982.

PDC *Prayers for the Domestic Church* by Edward Hays. Leavenworth, KS: Forest of Peace Books.

PsH *Psalter Hymnal.* Text by Calvin Seerveld, © 1986. Grand Rapids, MI: CRC Publications, 1987.

SMT *Proposed Services of Memorial and Thanksgiving.* Cleveland, OH: Office of Church Life and Leadership, United Church of Christ, © 1982.

TF *The Funeral: A Service of Witness to the Resurrection* (Supplemental Liturgical Resource 4). Philadelphia, PA: The Westminster Press, Copyright © 1986. Used by permission of Westminster/John Knox Press.

UCA *Uniting Church Worship Services: Funeral.* Melbourne: The Uniting Church in Australia Assembly Commission on Liturgy, © 1984. Used by permission of the Joint Board of Christian Education.

Pastoral Care at the Time of Death (pp. 21ff.)

Headings 1-11 are adapted from an article by Rev. Jim Kok published in the *Chaplain's Newsletter,* August, 1981, and *The Banner,* November 30, 1981.

Service of Prayer on the Occasion of a Miscarriage, Stillborn Child, or Early Death (pp. 63ff.)

This service was adapted from "A Service of Hope," copyright 1989 Christian Century Foundation. Reprinted by permission from the January-February 1989 issue of *The Christian Ministry,* p. 12.

The Ministry of the Congregation (pp. 213ff.)

The letter to the Congregation is based on "A Letter to the Clergy," written by Marchienne Rienstra, and published in *National Selected Morticians,* Autumn, 1977.